The Broken Road

The Broken Road

*George Wallace and a Daughter's
Journey to Reconciliation*

Peggy Wallace Kennedy
with Justice H. Mark Kennedy

BLOOMSBURY PUBLISHING
NEW YORK · LONDON · OXFORD · NEW DELHI · SYDNEY

BLOOMSBURY PUBLISHING
Bloomsbury Publishing Inc.
1385 Broadway, New York, NY 10018, USA

BLOOMSBURY, BLOOMSBURY PUBLISHING, and the Diana logo
are trademarks of Bloomsbury Publishing Plc

First published in the United States 2019

The photograph on page 144 is reprinted with permission
from AP Photo/Charles Kelly.

An excerpt from the article "Wallace's Rallies Blend Evangelism,
Music and Salesmanship" is reprinted on pp. 175–79 with
permission from the *New York Times*.

ISBN: HB: 978-1-63557-365-7; eBook: 978-1-63557-366-4

Library of Congress Cataloging-in-Publication Data
Names: Kennedy, Peggy Wallace, author. | Kennedy, H. Mark, author.
Title: The broken road / Peggy Wallace Kennedy with Justice H. Mark Kennedy.
Description: New York, NY : Bloomsbury Publishing, 2019. |
Includes bibliographical references and index.
Identifiers: LCCN 2019014085 | ISBN 9781635573657 (hardcover : alk. paper) |
ISBN 9781635573664 (eBook)
Subjects: LCSH: Kennedy, Peggy Wallace. | Kennedy, Peggy Wallace—Family. |
Wallace, George C. (George Corley), 19191998. | Children of governors—
Alabama—Biography. | Children of politicians—Alabama—Biography. |
Women—Alabama—Biography. | African Americans—Segregation—
Alabama—History—20th century. | Racism—United States—History—
20th century. | Alabama—Biography.
Classification: LCC F330.3.W34 K46 2019 | DDC 976.1/063092 [B]—dc23
LC record available at https://lccn.loc.gov/2019014085

2 4 6 8 10 9 7 5 3 1

Typeset by Westchester Publishing Services
Printed and bound in the U.S.A. by Berryville Graphics Inc., Berryville, Virginia

To find out more about our authors and books visit
www.bloomsbury.com and sign up for our newsletters.

Bloomsbury books may be purchased for business or promotional use.
For information on bulk purchases please contact Macmillan Corporate and
Premium Sales Department at specialmarkets@macmillan.com.

For my sons, Leigh and Burns.
I love you for the sons you are and the men you have become.
On those cracks and upheaved parts of the broken road where
we sometimes found ourselves living on,
you never left me standing there, all alone.
"Mom, over here, this way, there is a meadow of flowers
just over the hill.
Now, you hold our hands until we get there.
Don't you worry, if the dark of night falls 'round us,
we have a lantern to light the pathway home."

For my daughters-in-law, Stephanie and Hannah, amazing and
beautiful in their hearts.
You lift me up because you believe in me.
You inspire me with every sunrise.
And for that and for so much more,
I give you my love and heartfelt gratitude.

For my granddaughter, Maggie Rose.
A sometimes prickly but otherwise beautiful flower,
you bring me joy.
Your life of uncomplicated living challenges me to wonder.
When I am with you, nothing seems to be impossible.

You make me smile within this grandmother's heart of mine
when I hear
"I love you, Grandma Peggy."

For my husband, Mark.
Who oft reminds me,
What is a storm without thunder and lightning?
Rainbows following rain.
No climbing without holding on.
Without sunsets, no sunrises.
Without valleys, no mountains to climb.
No mending of hearts unless they are broken.
Love is different in times of our lives
and life can complicate things
but love, my dear, endures.

CONTENTS

FOREWORD

Anyone trying to make sense of our current divided America should read *The Broken Road*, Peggy Wallace Kennedy's wonderfully written memoir about the most famous political family in Alabama history. All the elements of white working-class rage that surged to the surface of American politics in 2016—working-class fury at social and education elites that they felt were demeaning them and their culture; economic and technological changes that overwhelmed them; immigrants whom they saw as competing for their low-wage jobs; religious "do-gooders" who seemed to emphasize justice for the poor while ignoring the old-time working-class gospels of hard work and "family values"—had emerged half a century earlier in Governor George C. Wallace's "politics of rage." As fate would have it, it may have been Arthur Bremer's failed 1972 assassination attempt, which left Wallace a paraplegic, that spared the nation a racist Democratic president whose campaigns first cultivated the rich nativist soil of "Stand Up for America" and "Make America Great Again."

Although historians and biographers have carefully narrated George Wallace's political career, they have not penetrated the inner sanctum of his closely guarded and dysfunctional family. In this deeply moving memoir, Peggy Wallace Kennedy depicts her mother, Lurleen Wallace, as a grand and noble figure, and her father as essentially an insecure, brilliant demagogue consumed by ambition. Always solicitous of white evangelicals and foregoing alcohol in public, they hid their hard liquor in the Governor's Mansion. While portraying himself as an example of traditional family values, George Wallace and his retinue of handlers carefully shielded from the public his neglect of family and legendary womanizing. And their children became casualties of parental ambition.

The Irish writer Oscar Wilde once wrote that "children begin by loving their parents; as they grow older they judge them; sometimes they forgive them." Readers of this memoir are fortunate that Peggy Wallace completed that entire life cycle—from childhood innocence to adult revulsion, to forgiveness, reconciliation, and finally to personal wholeness. The result may well be the most emotionally searing portrait ever written of an opportunistic American political demagogue, his threat to American values, and the tortured legacy he bequeathed his state, nation, and family. Among the readers, one might hope, would be the children and grandchildren of President Donald Trump, for one can easily imagine some distant Trump descendent wrestling with his legacy, and then going on to pen a similar exorcism of family demons.

—*Dr. Wayne Flynt, Professor Emeritus,*
Department of History, Auburn University

The Broken Road

1

The Bridge

In the South, we knew our adversary would stop at nothing to silence our activism. We knew we could never match his readiness to annihilate our resistance. So, we ceded to him that ground and challenged him instead to defend himself against the work of loving peace.

—*John Lewis*

I t was a sun-filled and breezy early spring day in Selma, Alabama, home to one of the most significant events of the civil rights era. Congressman John Lewis held my hand as we walked toward the Edmund Pettus Bridge, where in 1965 sheriff's deputies and Alabama State troopers had attacked the vanguard of approximately five hundred to six hundred people as they began a march for voting rights. The tempo of beating drums and our voices singing "We Shall Overcome" rode over and above the sound of our footsteps. John seemed oblivious to the disapproving eyes of some of those people who recognized me not for who I was but for what my father, George Wallace, had done in 1965 when he was governor of Alabama.

I had been asked to speak at the forty-fourth annual bridge crossing ceremony, commemorating what had come to be known as Bloody Sunday. After Bloody Sunday, the marchers had tried two more times to cross the bridge. It was only after President Lyndon B. Johnson and Attorney General Robert Kennedy federalized the Alabama National Guard to protect them that they succeeded. They walked for three days and then rallied at the capitol, which led to the passage of the historic Voting Rights Act of 1965.

My daddy had been a key player—on the wrong side—of this inspiring and heart-wrenching history. He publicly maintained that he had given an order to stop the marchers but not to harm them. He claimed that his deputy, Al Lingo, disobeyed. Even if this was true, though, he should have, at the very least, protected the marchers and their right to march. It would have been easy enough for him to issue an order to stop Lingo. Daddy's public denials that he had any part in what took place that day were like Pontius Pilate washing his hands.

I KNEW THAT I had to come to Selma following the inauguration of President Obama in January 2009. It wasn't easy for me. I had risked the disapproval of friends and family with my open support for Obama's candidacy, and I wondered if I dared to come before those who had suffered at the hands of my father in the 1960s and speak. It was a test of my courage. Would I be able to stand up and introduce America's first African American attorney general, Eric Holder? Holder's wife, Sharon, was the sister of Vivian Malone, who had met my father for the first time during another key event in the struggle for civil rights. Daddy had made his "stand in the schoolhouse door," as it came to be known, in June 1963, blocking Vivian's admission to the University of Alabama, which he had refused to desegregate. He infamously proclaimed: "Segregation now, segregation tomorrow, and segregation forever."

My husband, Mark, and I parked a few blocks from the church where I was slated to introduce Holder. Few recognized me as we walked through the streets, which were busy with people coming to commemorate the day, but as we approached the church's front doors, it became apparent word was spreading that George Wallace's daughter was going to be on the program.

Mark took a seat in the church while I was escorted to a small study to meet John Lewis and the legendary civil rights leader Joseph Lowery. I vividly remembered their heroic actions in Selma all those years before when I was just fifteen years old. I had sat beside my mother that night in the sitting room of the Governor's Mansion, watching *Judgment at Nuremberg* on TV, a film about the trial of German judges who had sentenced Jews under Hitler's regime.

"Weren't the Jews Germans too?" I asked.

"Yes," my mother replied.

The screen went blank and then came back on. Alabama state troopers and men on horseback chased a group of African Americans. A young man in a tan trench coat was bludgeoned and, on the ground, savagely beaten. I would learn that man's name was John Lewis.

My mother didn't outwardly react to the broadcast. She kept her feelings to herself, and so did I. But inside I was horrified. People were being beaten! How could my daddy allow that to happen? Bloody Sunday would haunt me and my family. My support of Obama and coming to Selma were part of my commitment to make things right. We must live our lives with inspiration, always aspiring to make the choices that lead us to higher ground, that guide us to understanding, of not just who we are but who we can become.

JOHN AND JOSEPH greeted me warmly. We talked about my father's later years, when he was crippled and in the twilight of his life and had renounced his former positions and tried to make amends. John, Joseph, and Jesse Jackson as well as other African American leaders had gathered at his bedside. He asked them for forgiveness—and they forgave him. What an incredible gift. And now they gathered me in the arms of collective friendship, and I felt all things were possible, and that indeed, in the words of Dr. Martin Luther King Jr., we would all cross over, cross over and reach the Promised Land.

John intimated that he understood the complexity of Daddy's character. He saw in him a conflicted man whose Achilles' heel had been his monomaniacal quest for power.

"I am from Pike County," John said.

"Well, I went to college at Troy State," I replied.

"I wanted to go to Troy State," John told me. "But I couldn't, so I called Dr. King to see if he could get me in. And Dr. King said,

'Why don't you just come and help me?'" That was the beginning of John's involvement in the civil rights movement.

It was impossible not to sense history when I entered the sanctuary of the Brown Chapel AME Church, a National Historic Landmark. It was from here that the voting rights march began. I was seated on the dais behind the pulpit with the others who would speak that day. The choir was behind us.

The sanctuary was full when the service began. For those who had lived through Bloody Sunday and its aftermath, what joy they must have felt to come to the very place where the voting rights march began, to celebrate the election of America's first African American president and see the first African American attorney general. As I walked to the lectern to introduce Holder, I felt my soul climb up beyond my fear of public speaking. I thought of my sons; it was a moment they could share with their children. I was there not because of who I was—the daughter of George and Lurleen Wallace—but rather for who I had become: a staunch advocate for civil rights and racial justice.

At the conclusion of the service, I stood arm in arm with Reverend Lowery and Jesse Jackson as we all sang "We Shall Overcome." We kept singing that anthem of the dream of freedom and equality for all people as we flowed out into the street and marched toward the bridge where the marchers had been met by sheriff's deputies and Alabama state troopers when I was just a girl.

The bridge loomed large in the distance. My hand was in John's hand. My voice rose with John's voice. We walked through the streets of Selma, once one of the wealthiest cities in the South, ringed by cotton plantations worked by slaves. I thought of another moment that had brought me to this point: November 5, 2008, the day after Barack Obama had been elected president. CNN had published an article I wrote in support of an Obama presidency. In it, I told the story of going to Greenwood Cemetery in Montgomery, where my parents were buried. I heard a car door slam behind me and turned to see an elderly but spry woman heading my way. The night before, a gang of vandals had swept through the cemetery desecrating graves, crushing head-stones and stealing funereal objects. My parents' graves, situated on a windswept hill overlooking the cemetery, had not been spared. A large marble urn that stood between two granite columns had been pried loose and spirited away, leaving faded silk flowers strewn on the ground.

I was holding a bouquet of them in my arms when the woman walked up and gave me a crushing hug. "Honey," she said, "you don't know me, but when I saw you standing up here on this hill, I knew that you must be one of the [Wallace] girls and I couldn't help myself but to drive up here and let you know how much me and my whole family loved both of your parents. They were real special people."

I thanked her for her kind words as we stood side by side gazing down at the graves of my parents. She leaned in to me with a conspiratorial whisper: "I never thought I would live to see the day when a black would be running for president. I know your daddy must be rolling over in his grave."

Not having the heart or the energy to respond, I gave her bony arm a slight squeeze, turned, and walked away. As I put the remnants of the graveyard sprig in the trunk of my car, I assumed that she had not noticed my Obama bumper sticker.

As a young voter, I'd had little interest in politics. Daddy marked my ballot for me. Leaving the cemetery, I mused that if Daddy were alive and I had made the same request for this election, there would be a substantial chance, though not a certainty, that he would have put an *X* by Obama's name. Perhaps Obama's election would have been the last chapter in the search for inner peace that became so important to him after becoming a victim of hatred and violence himself when he was shot and gravely injured in 1972.

The article on CNN.com had gotten 150,000 hits and brought me to national attention—here was obviously a very different kind of Wallace. And it was that article that led me to be invited to Selma for the anniversary of Bloody Sunday.

WITH HIS ARM around me, John and I stepped to the bridge's rail. "Peggy, crossing the bridge with you shows how far the human heart can go."

I finally felt I had fulfilled the promise I made to my son Burns when he was a nine-year-old. Mark and I had taken him to Atlanta to visit the Martin Luther King Jr. National Historic Site and Museum. As we moved through the exhibits, we turned a corner to face photographs of the Edmund Pettus Bridge, the bombed-out 16th Street Baptist Church, fire hoses and dogs in Birmingham, and Daddy standing in the schoolhouse door.

Burns turned to me. "Why did Paw Paw do those things to other people?" he asked.

I knelt beside Burns and drew him close. "Paw Paw never told me why he did those things to other people. But I do know that he was *wrong*. So maybe it will just have to be up to you and to me to help make things right."

It was really Burns's question that had compelled me to stand with John on the Edmund Pettus Bridge. It made me realize that I had to come to terms with my family's history. It awakened in me the deep desire to create my own chapter in the Wallace saga.

John and I stood together, watching the Alabama River flow beneath us. It was as if the water was reaching up to me, washing away the pain of the past and giving me courage to step away and find my true self.

"Well, sister," John finally said. "Guess it's time for the two of us to move forward. Now you hold my hand 'til we get to the other side."

2

In the Beginning

Family quarrels are bitter things. They don't go according to any rules. They're not like aches or wounds, they're more like splits in the skin that don't heal because there's not enough material.

—*F. Scott Fitzgerald*

Like many of us, I have often wondered how my parents came to be the people they were. They are gone now and their early lives and the lives of my grandparents and great-grandparents will always be a mystery to me. My parents didn't like to talk about their pasts. We were always so intent on pushing forward, focused on what was coming next.

My father's grandfather, Dr. George Oscar Wallace, arrived in Clio, Alabama, in 1891. He and his first wife moved into a wood-framed house across the street from the town's small collection of stores. He worked long hours, caring for ailing patients and tending to his drugstore in town. His meager success allowed him to build his own home, and he purchased three small tenant farms. His first wife died in 1920, and he later married Nora Mae Wyatt.

In my father's later years, Dr. Wallace and Mother Mae, as he called her, would be his touchstones. In his mind, there seemed to be no others sitting on the limbs of the family tree who could have passed along his intellect and ambition. Daddy's extended family members remained strangers, nothing more than awkward moments at campaign rallies or large family reunions where everyone bunched up to speak to the governor, ate, then left for parts unknown.

His parents were both, in their own ways, difficult people. My uncle Gerald laughingly characterized my grandfather George Wallace, Daddy's father, as "a man of indiscretion and perpetual drunkenness." My grandfather had gone to Southern University and returned home to Clio to manage his father's three farms. His endless hours of intoxication fueled his anger. He was prone to blinding headaches from a deviated septum, made worse when a friend hit him in the forehead with a pair of brass knuckles during a drunken brawl. With only one lung and a weak heart, George Wallace Sr., as described by one author, spent his days

Daddy in the first grade.

leaning on a counter in Clio's general store, a cigarette in one hand and a Coke in the other, ready to chase another headache powder.

When Daddy and his brothers, Gerald and Jack, were young boys, my grandfather would push the living room furniture up against the walls, roll up the rugs, and force the three boys to fight. The Clio telephone company was on the second floor of the building across the street and the operator could see right into Daddy's living room. On fight nights, the operator agreed to time the rounds and ring the Wallace phone when each was over. Sometimes she would ring the phone early when the fighting got out of hand. Most times that act of mercy didn't matter—a round was over when my grandfather said it was and not a moment sooner. On many nights the fight ended with my grandfather passed out drunk on the floor. When that happened, his wife, Mozelle, covered him with a blanket while her sons went off to lick their wounds.

AS I'VE GROWN older and raised two sons of my own, I have come to believe that the one person who had the greatest influence on what became the very complex and morose side of my father's psyche was his mother, Mozelle. Amid the stories of the Wallace clan, I sometimes wondered why there was nothing about Mozelle's family. It was as if she just appeared one day out of thin air. It was not until after her death that I found out the real story.

Mozelle was born in Ocala, Florida, in 1898. At the age of seven, she was living in Montgomery when her father suddenly died and the family fell into abject poverty. In 1906, when Mozelle was eight, her mother sent her to an Episcopal orphanage in Mobile, Alabama. Most of Mozelle's classmates at the school she attended were the Southern belles of Mobile. She was a gifted musician, and the Ladies' Episcopal Association of Mobile gave her a music scholarship to attend Judson College.

Mozelle's mother, Kate Leon Frink Smith, lived in Montgomery, then Birmingham until her death in 1968. She watched her grandson become governor and raised four of her greatgrandchildren. But we never knew she existed. No one mentioned her name. One of my cousins found her on Ancestry.com long after Mozelle had died. Was Mozelle's background kept secret from me or just deemed irrelevant? I don't know.

Mozelle Smith Wallace and George Corley Wallace.

After less than a year, Mozelle decided to leave Judson College. She had met my grandfather at a train station when she was on her way to school. Mozelle somehow discovered that George Wallace had left college and returned to Clio, and she followed him there and settled into a boardinghouse and gave piano lessons to the few children whose parents could afford to pay. Moving to Clio with the thought of snaring my grandfather was a long shot—an audacious plan. Mozelle pulled it off. It showed the force of her will, the kind of drive that she passed on to Daddy.

MY MOTHER'S UPBRINGING was very different from my father's. Her household was warm and loving. She was born on September 19, 1926, and lived in Northport, Alabama, just across the Black Warrior River from Tuscaloosa. The doctor who delivered her suggested the name Lurleen. Her father, Henry Burns, worked as a hand on coal barges. It took him away from home but provided more income than farming; for an uneducated man, it was about the best he could do. The Burns family often lived on the brink of poverty, but there was nothing to suggest that Lurleen and her older brother, Cecil, ever suffered the indignities of destitution.

My grandmother, Estelle Burns, whom I called Mamaw, ran the show. "Mr. Henry" was tenderhearted and gentle. My mother inherited my grandmother's backbone. After Mama was elected governor, she hung a framed quotation on the family dining room wall:

> A woman may be small of frame,
> With tiny feet that patter,
> But when she puts one small foot down,
> Her shoe size does not matter.

Those words were tailor-made for Mamaw and, my husband says, ruefully, me. Although Mama was of average height, I'm only four feet eleven, and Mamaw was also small. But don't let our size fool you.

Mr. Henry's sentimentality often brought him to tears. His love for his children exuded from every pore and his devotion to his daughter, Lurleen, was palpable. He nicknamed Lurleen "Mutt" in recognition of her determination to follow his every footstep, and he wept for her on the night she died.

AS I'VE ALREADY mentioned, my parents' accounts of their childhoods were spotty at best. Perhaps if I had been told more, it could have made a difference in who I became. Perhaps it would have made me love more. I felt an isolation within the family. It would have been wonderful to have bonds of affection with aunts and uncles, cousins, nieces, and nephews.

When our sons, Leigh and Burns, were young, Mark would drive them past the house he grew up in. There were no such places for me. The Clio house was destroyed by fire. Mr. Henry and Mamaw's place was abandoned, consumed by neglect. The house in Clayton that I grew up in burned to the ground. Sometimes I wonder if history is warning me never to look back, to let it rest and leave it alone. There was too much to know and nothing to cheer me up. There were no swings on front porches, only dark days and darker nights. No places to take my sons to show them how it was. Only graveyards with headstones: names and dates. That's all.

3

Romance in the Air

A line can be straight, or a street, but the human heart,
oh, no; it's curved like a road through the mountains.

—*Tennessee Williams*

B ut for the want of a bottle of hair tonic and a dare from a friend, my parents might never have met. There must have been something different about the young girl who sold Daddy a bottle of brilliantine at Kresge's five-and-dime in downtown Tuscaloosa, Alabama. Daddy asked his friend Glen Curlee if he knew the cashier's name. "Nope, but she's mighty cute," he replied. "She seems to be mighty young for the two of us."

"Well, I'm going to get a date with her," Daddy said.

Glen laughed. "Wallace, you don't even know her name."

"Tell you what. I'll bet you a quarter I can walk back inside right now and talk her into going out with me."

With money on the line, Daddy reentered the store and returned to the street within minutes. He put out his hand. "Time to pay up. Taking her to lunch tomorrow."

"What's her name?"

"Lurleen Burns."

It was the summer of 1942.

Daddy graduated from law school in the spring of 1942 and shortly thereafter was passing out cards to Tuscaloosa locals announcing that George C. Wallace, Esq., and Ralph Adams, Esq., had established a partnership for the purpose of practicing law in the City and County of Tuscaloosa. Freshly minted lawyers were abundant in Tuscaloosa, and when no clients came knocking, Daddy's financial situation became bleaker by the day. He persuaded a highway superintendent that he had great proficiency in driving dump trucks, although he had never driven one in his life.

The summer of 1942 must have seemed magical to my father as he rode a city bus almost daily from downtown Tuscaloosa across the Black Warrior River to Northport and on to Mama's house. With little money, the young couple spent most days in the

Mama when she was three years old.

Burnses' living room or on their front porch, always under the watchful eye of my grandparents. On occasion, my parents went to the movies in downtown Tuscaloosa or ate at one of the cheaper restaurants on the town's side streets. On Saturday, September 19, 1942, Mama and Daddy rode the bus from Northport into downtown Tuscaloosa to celebrate my mama's sixteenth birthday.

Mamaw was far from enthusiastic about Mama's new beau. He talked too much about being a lawyer and claimed that one day he was going to be governor of Alabama. His "nonsense" was just pie in the sky as far as Mamaw was concerned. "He talks like he's got a bucket of sugar in his mouth," she would say. Her disdain for Daddy was obvious. It didn't matter: Mama was smitten with the young swaggart, despite his gaudy taste in shirts, his threadbare pants, and his slicked-back hair.

In February 1943, Daddy received his induction notice and left Northport for basic training in South Florida. From there, he reported to the Air Force Cadet Training Program in Arkadelphia, Arkansas.

My mamaw used to say, "Well, when George shipped out to Arkansas to learn how to fly a plane, I thought that was going to be that and Lurleen would get back on track. And then just my luck, the boy got spinal meningitis, almost died but didn't, then here he comes, not to his mama, but back on *our* front porch."

Mama never thought that story was funny, but I did. I loved to hear Mamaw tell it. Mama would chime in: "George only weighed a hundred and twenty-two pounds when he came back. Before he left Arkansas, he was in a coma for almost a week. When he finally got well enough to be put on leave, he had to ride a train all by himself to Tuscaloosa." She would sometimes say to Mamaw, "Mama, you are making all of this up."

Mamaw would usually reply, "Well, he talked you into marrying him, didn't he?"

Mamaw's somewhat comical disdain for Daddy was a great source of amusement to my family—she really had his number. My father's fidgeting, his endless verbiage, and his born-for-politics personality chafed against her clear-eyed common sense and down-to-the-bones morality. "For sure, that boy can't sit still," was about all Mr. Henry would say.

ON SATURDAY, MAY 22, 1943, less than a week after Daddy returned, he and Mama were wed. With Mamaw in tow, Mama and Daddy went to the office of a Jewish justice of the peace, but not before Mamaw signed a form giving her underage sixteen-year-old daughter consent to be married.

Following the ceremony, Mama, Daddy, Mamaw, and the justice of the peace enjoyed a meal of chicken salad sandwiches and Cokes at Ward's. Mamaw gave Mama and Daddy a hug before they boarded a train to Montgomery so that Mama could meet her mother-in-law, Mozelle.

In 1937, when Daddy was a freshman at the University of Alabama, his father died. Daddy left college and returned to Clio to help Mozelle survive. She was selling the family farms to satisfy their outstanding mortgages. Not long after Daddy arrived, she told him to pack his things up and go back to Tuscaloosa and stay in school. She would manage. After Gerald and Jack graduated from high school, Mozelle sold the Clio house, and she and my aunt

Marianne moved to Montgomery. She got a job with the State Health Department and settled into a two-bedroom apartment.

That was where my newlywed parents were going. It was after nightfall when the train pulled into Union Station in Montgomery. Daddy hailed a cab and gave the driver Mozelle's address. Mozelle was not aware that Daddy was back in Alabama on medical leave, recovering from spinal meningitis. She was obviously surprised when she opened her front door to find Daddy, haggard and worn from his recent illness, holding hands with a teenage girl.

What happened that night never ceases to amaze me: it indicates just what kind of person my grandmother was. Daddy introduced Mama as his bride. After what seemed to be an eternity and without acknowledging Mama's presence, Mozelle raised her head and looked up at Daddy, and said, in the same dispassionate voice that Daddy knew growing up, "I thought you would have done better than this."

When I think about that story, I'm conflicted. As a mother of two sons myself, I wonder what my reaction would have been had I opened that door and found one of my sons, who I thought was in a military hospital in another state, standing at my door next to a teenage girl I had never seen, and then hearing that she was his wife. It was a lot to absorb. But as my mother's daughter, I wonder why Daddy didn't stand up for Mama.

Mozelle's opinion of Mama never wavered from that point—even when my mother became governor. Her belief that Daddy could have done better never changed.

After a brief visit, Daddy took Mama to the boardinghouse in downtown Montgomery. The rooms were small and dingy with a single lightbulb hanging from the ceiling, casting shadows on a cracked linoleum floor. One bathroom at the end of the hall on the second floor served all.

Maybe Mama didn't even notice that the surroundings were shabby. After all, she was sixteen years old and in the arms of the man she loved.

BETWEEN 1943 AND the spring of 1945, Mama shuttled back and forth between Daddy's duty stations and Alabama. Their first daughter, Bobbie Jo, was born. During my father's last stateside posting, Mama arrived at the train station in Alamogordo, New Mexico. The Army air field where Daddy was stationed was approximately fifteen miles away.

When she got there, she realized that Daddy had not bothered finding them a place to live. They walked up and down streets, looking for somewhere to rent or at least bed down. Night fell and the temperature dropped. Daddy persuaded a stranger to allow them to sleep on his screened-in front porch. For three nights they lay on a bare wooden floor with their newborn daughter between them, then spent three more weeks in a small rented room until Daddy proudly announced to Mama that he had found the perfect place, a small two-room chicken coop that had been converted into a barely livable shanty with concrete floors, electricity, and a kerosene stove. With no insulation and holes in the lean-to roof, Mama constantly battled blowing sand and shivered at night in the high-altitude air that was constantly on the move.

AFTER THE CESSATION of hostilities in Europe, the world's eye focused on the war with Japan. In preparation for delivering a death blow, thousands of Army Air Force personnel, pilots, and flight crews deployed to the Pacific. On July 19, 1945, Daddy, who had been trained as a flight engineer, flew on a mission to bomb the Japanese city of Fukui. His plane was caught in a thermal updraft caused by rising heat from the thousands of firebombs that had already been dropped. The plane shot up from 12,800 feet to 18,000 feet in a matter of seconds and stalled. The aircraft plummeted toward the water, but Daddy was able to restart one of the crippled engines. They regained altitude and turned home.

The exhausted crew fell asleep. By the time they awakened they had wandered one hundred and fifty miles off course. There was not enough fuel to make it back to their base, and the consensus was that they were going to have to land the aircraft in the sea. My father refused to consider that possibility, nursing the shrinking fuel reserve. When the plane landed at Tinian, the crew cheered. Daddy was a hero but terribly shaken.

Later in life, Daddy refused to talk about the incendiary bombs they dropped on Japan. Nor would he talk about August 5. In the late afternoon, his aircraft departed Tinian on its ninth and final mission. Just as the sun was rising on the east horizon, Daddy's aircraft crossed the flight path of the *Enola Gay* as it flew toward Hiroshima.

IN DECEMBER 1945, Daddy was hired as an assistant attorney general in Montgomery, making $175 a month. A day job and a modest wage was a real first step to settling down, perhaps in a modest home, my mother thought. However, in March 1946, Daddy took a leave from the attorney general's office to run for the Alabama legislature from Barbour County. My parents moved to Clayton. Upon his election at the age of twenty-seven, he became the youngest legislator in the history of Alabama. And Mama and Daddy's finances once again fell into ruin.

The legislature was a part-time job, poorly paid, and they met only every other year for five months. When it was out of session, Daddy was home and unemployed. Perhaps he tried to practice law. More likely, he spent his time going here and there, politicking and ingratiating himself. Mama was once again forced to be the breadwinner and parent. She did secretarial work and had no choice but to move back to the run-down boardinghouse where she spent the first night of her marriage. When the legislature recessed, she returned to Clayton, living in the attic of an elderly woman's house.

Mama lived in poverty for almost a decade. She would die when I was eighteen, and I never really got to ask her about this period. I don't think my mother could have been amused by my father's total disregard for their comfort. Daddy would sometimes reminisce about the days when he and Mama were young and carefree. "We had the world on a string," he said. "Those were good times." Daddy could justify anything. He was always blameless should things go wrong. He led a don't-blame-me kind of life.

4

Coming Home

It's like building a nest. First, she thinks about it, then she begins to gather the materials, then she begins to put it together.

—*Flannery O'Connor*

I was born on January 24, 1950, in Eufaula, Alabama—twenty miles or so from Clayton. Daddy had left the legislature and become a circuit court judge.

My aunt Betty Jean Wallace, a Southern belle from Baker Hill, Alabama, who married Daddy's youngest brother, Jack, was in Mama's hospital room when Mamaw and Mr. Henry arrived. Aunt Betty Jean loved to tell the story of that day: "Honey, I was standing by the door when Estelle and Mr. Henry busted in the door. Almost knocked me down. The first thing Estelle spied was your daddy. 'Well,' she said, 'look who showed up. Did you get here in time to see the baby get born? That would be a *no*, I bet.'

"Your daddy took that cigar out of his mouth, kissed you on the top of your head, gave your mother a peck on the cheek, and out the door he went. Then here he comes again. 'Sugah, you call me if you need anything,' he said. 'I'll get back to you just as fast as I can.'

" 'I wouldn't hold my breath!' Estelle said. She just couldn't stand it. But we all just laughed and laughed."

That was my father, perpetually in motion. Focused on one thing: politics, politics, politics. That was just the way he was—always on the move. He talked fast, ate fast, and was the first out the door, calling to the rest of us: "Y'all come on, it's time to go." As long as Daddy had enough food to keep him going, a shirt pocket full of cigars, and an occasional manicure, he was set. He didn't care about where he lived, or what he ate (as long as it had ketchup on it), or where he slept—he was oblivious to creature comforts.

I WAS BROUGHT home to Clayton. Before we bought it, our Clayton house was chopped up into three apartments. We lived in the dining room, shared a bathroom with two other families, and had kitchen privileges.

My father might have kept living that way indefinitely, but my mother prevailed. We purchased the property and took over the whole space. The house was not as grand as some of Clayton's older homes, but it had a wide front porch and high ceilings. The large trees in the oversized yard offered plenty of shade. Peeling paint, a leaking roof, and dark interiors begged for attention. Mama did most of the fixing up herself. Daddy had neither the time nor the interest. He swooped in and out, always on the move.

When Daddy was not at the courthouse, "adjudicating," as he would say, he was mostly in Montgomery, hobnobbing with the "movers and shakers," as he called them. These were men who hung out at the Exchange and Jefferson Davis hotels.

After Mama renovated the Clayton house, she became more confident in herself. She got a part-time job and began to spread her wings with friends. We joined the Methodist Church, although she had been raised Baptist. Daddy was a Methodist, and back then when you married you joined your husband's church. She even persuaded Daddy to buy her a secondhand baby grand piano for the living room. On some summer days, passersby might have heard a halting version of "Carolina Moon" floating through the white organza curtains covering the open porch windows.

It was during these years that Mama became lifelong friends with some of the women who would follow her to Montgomery after Daddy was elected governor. Her best friend was Mary Jo Ventress, a home economics teacher whose husband was a banker and small-town entrepreneur. A narrow lane and a hedgerow separated our house from the high school where Mary Jo taught. During her planning periods at school, Mama would often join Miss Mary Jo in her classroom to share a cup of coffee and catch up on the news. Mary Jo would remain by Mama's side up to the moment Mama died in the Governor's Mansion in 1968.

My mother was relatively content during those years—she had a home, family, friends, and respect. But Daddy seethed with ambition. There was always a sense that it would be just a matter of time before we would pull up stakes and move on. To him, a house was not a home, just a place of convenience where you went to get ready to go somewhere else.

He was restless at home and unhappy in his job. The duties and community expectations of a circuit judge were not his style. He dreamed of real power, and the country courthouses of Barbour and Bullock counties became like prisons to him.

Yet by all accounts he fairly and responsibly discharged his duties as a judge. He was well liked by the African American community. He was known for ensuring that African American lawyers who appeared before him were treated with deference, were addressed as *Mister*. He often invited them to eat with him in his office rather than suffer the indignity of eating in the segregated restaurant on the courthouse square. African American attorneys reported that Judge Wallace, down in Barbour County, was one of the fairest judges in Alabama.

It may surprise some people to learn that after being elected to the Alabama House of Representatives at the age of twenty-seven, Daddy became known as a progressive—and some said a liberal—Alabama Democrat. In his first legislative session, Daddy introduced more than forty bills to fund programs for the poor, paid for by higher taxes on the wealthy. In 1947, he introduced legislation that when passed became known as the Trade School Act. In 1949 and 1951, he and a fellow legislator co-authored the Wallace-Cater Act, allowing municipalities and counties to use their revenues to create industrial parks and attract industry. He regularly railed against large corporations and blocked legislation to raise the sales tax, which he referred to as "sock it to the poor" legislation. In 1951, Daddy asked Governor Jim Folsom to appoint him to the Board of Trustees of the Tuskegee Institute, founded by Booker T. Washington and at the time one of the most prestigious African American colleges in the South. During his two-year tenure, he often proposed programs to elevate the college's public profile and expand its curriculum. He never missed a Board of Trustees meeting during his term. His dedication to Tuskegee belied his coming to the politics of segregation in the decade to follow.

Daddy's service as a trustee at Tuskegee Institute in the early 1950s, and his respectful and judicious interactions with African American attorneys and their clients, was an interesting footnote to the scholars and historians who grappled with the complexity of Daddy's character. Yet this was who he was . . . and then was not. For Daddy was willing to bend his moral universe toward power. As I would learn again and again in sometimes painful ways, he was ready to compromise not only himself but his family for the dream he had since he was a child—to be the governor of Alabama.

DURING THE STIFLINGLY hot and humid summers of central Alabama there wasn't much going on in the courthouses. Jury terms would not pick back up until after Labor Day. There were non-jury cases, a few divorces, and the weekly docket calls to make sure that anyone who was locked up the week before had a chance to apply for bail. It was mostly about county roustabouts getting out of control. Family members would appear on our front porch to ask Daddy for mercy and to set the miscreant free.

"It was just a big ol' misunderstanding," most would say. "Things got out of control, and that gun just fired and, you know, shit just happens." After a tongue-lashing, Daddy would often release the offender to a "responsible party." While he preferred that people think that he was hard on crime, he had a soft spot for people who were born with no chance. People never accused Daddy of being a softie; they just thought he was fair-minded.

DADDY'S WORKDAYS, WHICH meant any time that he was not at home, were commonly twelve to thirteen hours long. When he wasn't in the courtroom, he could most times be found sitting on the courthouse steps or leaned up against a corridor wall conversing with lawyers, townsfolk, and perfect strangers. Although it might have been years between a person's first encounter with Daddy and the second, Daddy never forgot a face and a name. It was uncanny—a powerful tool in his political bag of tricks that he would become famous for.

The manacles of restraint, self-discipline, and dignity Daddy dragged around under his black robe ran counter to his nature. A passion for fighting and huckstering oozed from his pores. Circuit court judge was the only job Daddy would ever have that required him to face a crowd and let other people talk while he just listened. He also had to let a group of twelve people decide how things were going to turn out. Then, at the end of the day, his family expected him to come home and be happy to be there.

It was well known that my father had a wandering eye. Miss Mary Jo told me much later in life that Mama was not the only wife in Clayton whose husband "sought adventure elsewhere," as

Mary Jo would say. "But honey, when your mother caught on, there was going to be a big price to pay."

Mary Jo was referring to one of my favorite stories about my mother: the Case of the White Cadillac.

WEDNESDAY AFTERNOON WAS deemed a half day of rest and repose for commercial establishments in small towns like Clayton, Alabama. It was as much a Southern tradition as refraining from going to the picture show or ironing clothes on Sundays. Windows were shuttered at noon on Main Street, and only a small workforce remained in the clerk's office in the court-house where Daddy's office was. By early afternoon, the comings and goings around the courthouse square went pretty much unnoticed. That is, unless you were driving a white Cadillac with a red leather interior.

Miss Mary Jo told me the story in her thick Alabama drawl: "Back in those days, anything as unusual as a white Cadillac parked downtown on a Wednesday afternoon would certainly draw atten-tion, which then always led to speculation. So the talk goes out that George was holding court by himself on Wednesday afternoons. That didn't take long to get back to Lurleen. All she had to do was stand in the middle of the street in front of your house to have a bird's-eye view of the courthouse. And sure enough, Wednesday afternoons, just like clockwork, here came that white Cadillac.

"One Wednesday, she picked me up in that dark green worn-out Chevrolet Bel Air of hers and we went and parked on the other side of the Confederate monument in front of the courthouse. Oh, honey, that Cadillac had trouble written all over it. Lurleen and I called it the *something's up car* and we were right. After a while, there was so much smoke from Lurleen's cigarettes in that car, I got out and walked over to Seale's Café to get a glass of water. Just as I stepped back out on the sidewalk, I see a woman in a 'too tight to wear to church' blue dress with a clutch purse under an arm that had so many bracelets on it that it was a wonder the poor woman could even bend her elbow. Her hair was so teased up you could tell she was a regular at some high-class beauty parlor wherever she came from.

"Lurleen had the car running and was waving me to hurry up. We followed that Cadillac right through town, past the cemetery and the church. We fell back a bit once we hit the highway. Well, here comes a hill so we just flew on past her. Then Lurleen pulled into the middle of the road and starts pumping the brakes. I still get a neckache just thinking about it. It was going to be either pull over or get run over. The poor woman pulled over on the shoulder of the road and just sat there, 'wide-eyed and terrified' as we used to say.

"Lurleen got out and walked back to that poor woman's car and invited her to step outside, but she wasn't going to budge. That is until Lurleen went back and opened the trunk of our car and pulled out a tire iron. 'Surely she is not going to bust out that woman's windshield,' I said to myself. And, for the most part, I was right. Soon the entire hood of that poor woman's car looked like a crushed-up can of sardines. She finally opened the door and began babbling like a brook. On and on she went, just a poor damsel in distress and Judge Wallace was just trying to help a damsel in distress.

"Needless to say, Lurleen decided to follow in your daddy's footsteps and help that woman, who, at that point, was indeed and entirely in distress. Lurleen's assistance and advice was such that I assume she never came back to Clayton, or if she did, it was not in that white Cadillac."

MY FATHER'S GENERATION of politicians was not the last that felt the need to physically and mentally overpower women. That kind of behavior seems to be more often about power than pleasure, boosting the ego of insecure men who find themselves powerless in other ways.

Daddy was notorious for enjoying the company of women. He craved their attention and adoration. Throughout his life, it was more important to Daddy to be recognized than it was to be truly valued. Uncle Gerald used to explain it best when he talked about his and Daddy's father: "When we were growing up, Daddy used to tell us, 'Now you boys just remember, it's more important that you got where you wanted to go, rather than what you had to do to get there along the way.' It makes life a whole lot easier, thinking that way."

Although much has been written about Daddy, my uncle Gerald Wallace has not been given his full due. He was the glue that held the Wallace clan together. Although there were times when Daddy disparaged him in public, Uncle Gerald was Daddy's last resort. He was the family fixer, the go-between for making things right, Mama's advocate when Daddy was on the warpath or flailing around when he was cornered. Uncle Gerald was

Mozelle's favorite son. He was a raconteur and rascal, a hard-drinking and conniving man you couldn't help but love.

After Uncle Gerald and Daddy came home from the war, Gerald was down on his luck. He had contracted tuberculosis slogging through jungle trails and crawling through rice paddies in the Solomon Islands. He spent two years in military hospitals. By the time he was discharged in 1947, he had lost one lung and a wife. Over the course of the following seven or eight years, he was in and out of sanatoriums and veterans' homes. When a second wife divorced him, Gerald headed to our house in Clayton. "You can come stay with us until you get on your feet, and that better be quick," Daddy told his brother.

Uncle Gerald was a smallish man with skin that hung loosely from a bony frame. He had a shock of Wallace hair and dark piercing eyes always covered by black-framed sunglasses. He couldn't have weighed more than one hundred and twenty pounds soaking wet. He drank beer and whiskey, smoked Lucky Strikes, and wore hand-me-down clothes. Most of the grownups in town called him Sag.

Uncle Gerald usually stayed in a worn-out plaid bathrobe, held together by one of Daddy's frayed belts, until late morning. He dressed for lunch. In the afternoon he and Mama shared smokes on the backdoor steps and on some days enjoyed an occasional late afternoon cocktail, when whiskey was available.

Whiskey was a hard-to-find commodity in a dry county (a county where the preachers and the bootleggers round up people and haul them to the polls to vote no on a referendum on whether not liquor can legally be sold or consumed in that county). Not only was Barbour County dry—Daddy was a judge, and you can see how difficult it would have been for Mama and Uncle Gerald to enjoy cocktail hour at our house in Clayton. But then, nothing is impossible.

On many occasions Mama asked Daddy to buy a bottle of bourbon when he was in Montgomery and bring it back to Clayton. Sometimes he would but most times not. "You two are going to get me beat next time I run," he'd warn his brother and wife before handing the liquor over.

UNCLE GERALD LEFT Clayton to go to law school at the University of Alabama in 1957. I was seven years old and my

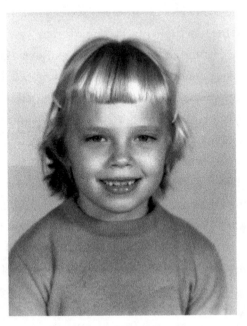

My first-grade school picture.

brother, George, was five. My mama was probably sorry to see him go. If there was ever a man that Mama counted on other than Daddy, it was Uncle Gerald. Perhaps, in some ways, he was more her type: slow to anger, always had time to talk. There never was a physical attraction between the two, but Gerald empathized with Mama, listened to her, and made her feel that she had value. He was the family peacemaker and, when required, most likely to succeed in getting Daddy off his "high horse." On more than one occasion, I remember Mamaw saying to Mama, "If I were you, I'd pick up that phone right this minute and call Gerald."

I'VE PAINTED A picture of my father as a man with one foot out the door. That is not entirely true. He loved us and enjoyed being with us, and the times I spent with him when he was occasionally in the frame of mind to be a father were glorious. Daddy never slipped into a room quietly so as not to disturb. He flung doors open with a presence that was vibrant, crackling with energy, and impulsively affectionate, hugging me fiercely and tousling my hair. We watched the Saturday night boxing matches together when he was at home, with rowdy commentary from both of us. Daddy had been a two-time Alabama Golden Glove champion and captain of the boxing team at the University of Alabama.

There was never a time that I can remember that he did not have a small bag of M&M's in his right-hand suit coat pocket for me—a consumable token of his love. But in return, there were certain conditions. I needed to behave in a certain way. "Honey, now you need to smile," he would say. Our relationship was based on *his* needs, not mine. I never doubted his love for me, but I never experienced those moments between a father and daughter when just being together was enough. He was there and then he was gone, and even when he was present I rarely felt that he gave me his undivided attention.

After Mark and I were married, there were times when I would become unsettled listening to his family reminisce. They sometimes invited me to share memories. Mark asked me why the stories I told were usually about my parents with less or even nothing about me. I guess I assumed I just wasn't very interesting. I didn't express my thoughts and feelings and opinions—Daddy never asked for them. In fact, until I had children of my own, I didn't realize that that kind of attention on his part *should* have been part of my life. I believed my mama when she said to me, "Peggy Sue, your daddy loves us, but this is just the way he is."

In 1988, Mark ran a statewide race for a seat on the Alabama Supreme Court. The campaign was an uphill battle—there were thousands of hands to shake, money to raise, sixty-seven courthouse walk-throughs and rallies, long nights on the road. Our son Leigh was nine years old, and I was pregnant with our second son, Burns.

One evening I found Leigh lying on the bed in his room. He was facing the wall. I could tell he was crying. I walked in and sat down beside him, putting my hand on his shoulder. "What's wrong?" I asked.

He turned toward me. "I miss Daddy. I wish he would come home."

I leaned in close. "I understand," I said. "I know you do."

Leigh looked at me in thought for a moment then raised up on his elbows in the bed. "You do know how it feels, don't you, Mama?"

His words pierced my heart.

MY MAMA WOULD put her foot down, and we did occasionally have what today would be called some "quality" family time. In the summer of 1957, we vacationed in a small wooden bungalow several blocks back from the water's edge in Panama City Beach, Florida. Mama loved to fish, swim in the Gulf, and beach-sit for hours. It was the perfect place for her, but not for Daddy. No phone and nowhere of particular interest to politick soon became a carbuncle on my father's rear end. His misery was infectious, although he tried mightily to feign fun times for the sake of the rest of us. There were no walks on the beach or building sand-castles with Daddy. Even when he went to the beach he wore dress shoes and a short-sleeved white shirt and tie.

One night, as a token of goodwill, Daddy agreed to take us to a beachside carnival. I was excited. It would be the first time in my life that all of us had done something together.

It was a miraculous night. The fair was all whirling lights—a garden of delights for a seven-year-old. Upon seeing the Bullet Ride, I felt emboldened and insisted that Daddy and I throw caution to the wind and go on it. After some whining and begging, Daddy consented.

The Bullet consisted of two metal cage-like structures, both attached to the ends of a metal arm that could rotate 360 degrees.

After we got buckled in with what appeared to be nothing more than a man's broad leather work belt, a swinging motion commenced. Confident that this was as bad as it would get, Daddy encouraged me to wave to Mama. He patted my knee and smiled. "Here we go, Uudlum Scuudlum," he chirped. When it became apparent we were about to go over and around, Daddy tensed and gripped the sides of the metal cage. By the time we had made one complete revolution, he was white as a sheet. "You are scaring my daughter," he yelled to the carnival worker. "Stop this damn thing now!" The growl of the smoked-up diesel engine powering the ride drowned out his demands. My mama was standing nearby smoking a cigarette and laughing. She finally had him where she wanted him, caged up and panic-stricken.

When the ride came to a stop and the door of the cage opened, Daddy's Brylcreemed hair was akimbo. "You shouldn't let children ride this thing," he said to the carnival worker, scrambling around the cage to collect the contents of his pockets. Then he stepped from the platform and threw up all over his scuffed-up Sunday shoes. This put my mama into stitches. And the more she laughed, the more infuriated he became. He had never been gracious about being the brunt of a joke.

Warm salt air rushed through the open windows of the car as Mama drove us back to the cottage. "Cut the giggling, Lurleen," Daddy said. His head was in his lap. "Pull over. I'm gonna vomit. That damn thing should be illegal. If one of those coupler ties had broken, we could have been flung across the entire beach and into the water. You should have never let me, much less your daughter, get on such a murderous contraption." On and on he went—even in his sorry condition, my father wasn't at a loss for words. The next morning, we packed up, helped Daddy to the car, emptied an ice tray into a beach towel for his head, and went home.

The next time I saw a Bullet Ride was at the Alabama State Fair in Montgomery. I was the mother holding the stuffed animal prizes, and my son and his friend were swinging in the metal cage. The Bullet Ride I took with Daddy in the summer of 1957 returned to me as a parable. It was a lesson learned of what a man like my father, who always had to be in control at all times, becomes when that control is wrested from him. It unmasked an ultimate truth—the deep insecurities that were behind his bravado.

I sometimes forget that as a child, Daddy grew up in a house of rage, where his alcoholic father was violent and out of control. His mother refused to fight back for herself or for her children. Daddy's tempestuous spirit always sat on the tip of his tongue. Perhaps it was always ready in case his insecurities attempted an escape. There are those who admire politicians who focus their energy on power rather than compassion, whose words spark anger and fear rather than the reconciliation and peace for which we all deeply yearn.

The politics of today plays to that same sense of fear and anger. Make America Great Again is not a plan. It is an insinuation that America is not good enough to be proud of. It is a pledge of allegiance to discrimination. It makes people feel that their way of life is under assault, and their deepest values are being trampled, no matter how misguided, hurtful, or destructive those notions are. It makes hating *right*.

In 1957, when we lived in Clayton and I rode the Bullet Ride with Daddy, the angry face of history had yet to show itself to me. But show itself it eventually did, and I knew I had to do everything I could to advance another vision of who we are and what we stand for. It is John Lewis's "work of loving peace," and that work is ongoing and as vital today as it was when my father threw up on his Sunday shoes. As I write this I hear my daddy say, "Uudlum Scuudlum, you're doing just fine. I sure am proud of you."

5

The Race

If I can't treat a black man fairly, I don't deserve to be governor.

—*George Wallace*

Daddy's departure from the Alabama house of representatives and his election as a circuit judge were calculated steps toward the governor's race in 1958. Daddy needed a position of influence and a lot of free time to roam around and politick. According to his biographers, he spent much of the time he wasn't adjudicating—hours and hours—in the lobbies of the Exchange and Jefferson Davis hotels, ingratiating himself to passersby. And while he was running for governor, Uncle Jack could run for the seat on the circuit court Daddy was vacating. Two Barbour County Wallaces on the ballot at the same time would pile up votes for both brothers.

During the early years of his political life, Daddy had been for the most part ignored by the "highbrows," as he called the men who inherited a fortune rather than earned one. "They are the ones that hold their pinky finger straight out when they take a drink of whiskey at the country club," he would say. Although he had mostly contempt for their good fortune, he made it a point to ply them with an aggressive and sometimes fawning attitude, the proverbial fox in the henhouse. They misjudged him. To them he was just another small-time politician from south Alabama who was always running around trying to find a hand to shake.

In March 1958, in front of the county courthouse in Clayton, Daddy announced that he was running for governor. Although it was a straight shot of less than three blocks from our house, we drove—Mama and Daddy up front, my brother and sister and me in back. The town square in front of the courthouse was packed with Wallace supporters from Clio, Eufaula, Midway, Union Springs, and the countryside. The Clayton high school band began to play and majorettes twirled batons as our car approached. Farmers with weatherworn faces and country women with their arms folded over Sunday dresses belted at the waist made up most of the crowd, along with a few women in fashionable summer frocks and men in business suits. Our maid, Bernice, stood with the black men, women, and children gathered on the periphery.

We all stood behind Daddy on a flatbed trailer spanning the width of the courthouse steps. U.S. flags, Alabama state flags, and Confederate flags rustled in the sighs of a spring breeze. The central square in Clayton, like the center of most towns in Alabama, had a monument—a statue of a Confederate soldier, facing north.

The sound of stomping and cheering emanated from the hyped-up crowd. The unbridled and unruly energy of their adoration made me uneasy. It was as though they were "pitching a fit," as Aunt Betty Jean would say. Daddy knew how to roust people up, make them shout and raise fists. Women fanned themselves with their hands as if they were in the middle of a hot flash.

"He's just good old people like us. Don't put on no face, puts his pants on one leg at a time. Grew up just like us," Daddy's people would always say. "You know his daddy drank himself to death. His poor mama, Mozelle, she just sat there and took it, doing the best she could."

Daddy stood transfixed as the mood of the crowd enveloped him. He had waited all of his life for a moment like this.

Holding his hands up, Daddy stepped close to the microphone. His speech started out with God and country. "Us small-town country folks deserve a voice just like those rich folks that think they are better than us," he said. Class warfare and, years later, race warfare were Daddy's aces in the hole—the source of his power. His cadence began to pick up as his forefinger and voice stabbed the air. I felt the power of his oratory, although I didn't pay much attention to what was being said. Our instructions were to stand quietly. Don't fidget! Mama smiled, applauding when she thought it was necessary. There were no visual cues or nods toward us to let us know what to do. I stood straight with my hands clasped in front of me. Daddy's speech ended abruptly. "God bless the great state of Alabama," he cried. The crowd stood still as if stunned. Then roars of approval rose up and floated up and over us. People moved toward us with hands outstretched and eyes filled with adulation. The band played "Dixie." Mama stepped up beside Daddy, and they both bent over with their hands outstretched. Volunteers passed out bumper stickers and collected donations (mostly pocket change) in metal buckets. Seale's Café, across the street from the courthouse, set up card tables with punch and cookies.

From somewhere behind me, our maid, Bernice, called my name. "I'll take you back to the house," she said. I held her hand as she navigated us through the crowd. An African American woman waved and called out to Bernice. "Bernice! You tell Judge Wallace if black folks could vote, we would be voting for him." The reason black folks couldn't vote was because of Jim Crow laws. They were systemically disenfranchised (and still are). Many African Americans in the South became disheartened and gave up trying to register to vote. They knew the deck was stacked against them by literacy tests and the requirement to produce certain forms of ID and other arbitrary barriers set up by the local boards of politically appointed registrars.

Nevertheless, Bernice was proud and moved to be working for a man who was running for governor. It's *always* complicated in the South.

Bernice was short and stocky. Her hand in mine felt weatherworn. Her round face was placid. Her body and the way she moved were more expressive than what she said. "Now you have to yell for me to hear you," Bernice would sometimes remind me. Her hearing loss was a result of the beatings her mother, Eva, gave to her when she was a child.

Her relationship to our family was typical across the South. Bernice had a daughter named Alice and a grandson named Tommy. Around the time my father announced for governor, I remember being awakened in the middle of the night. Bernice was at the door with Tommy, who was perhaps two or two and a half years old, in her arms. He had a fever and was in pain from an ear infection. Mama took Tommy from Bernice and rocked him through the night. Mama, Bernice, and Tommy were at the doctor's office before it opened the next morning. On the way back home, Mama stopped at the drugstore and paid for the medicine the doctor prescribed.

I loved Bernice. During summers, I spent more daylight hours with her than with Mama and Daddy. From Monday to Fridays and sometimes on Saturday mornings, Bernice took care of us and listened to what we said. On most weekday afternoons, she covered the food for supper on the stove with a clean dishrag, gathered up her purse and sometimes a paper bag with food or things Mama had given her, and disappeared out the back door to walk home or ride with Mama when it rained. In the confines of our house on Eufaula Street, Bernice felt like a second mother to me. After we left Clayton for the last time in December 1961, I never saw Bernice again.

Now I look back on my childhood with Bernice from a different viewpoint, relating to the culture of paternalism toward African Americans during that time. "They were just like family," we said.

Some would say that paternalism is just a softer version of racism, but in truth there is no difference. And sometimes it is even worse than harder-edged bigotry (we have plenty of that kind too). What I know is that in the age we live in now, a compassionate America seems in mortal danger. The Edmund Pettus Bridge still stands. But we, it seems, have regressed.

———

THE MEMORY OF my mama rocking Tommy as Bernice asked her, "Is he going to be all right?"—and African American men and women sometimes knocking on our front door to talk to Daddy about locking someone up or getting someone out—is conflated in my memory with an encounter with an African American seamstress from around this time.

Mama handed me several items of clothes that needed mending and gave me directions to the seamstress's house in the colored section of town. I found my way there, and as I climbed the steps of the front porch, I heard a woman's voice coming from inside the house. "George Wallace don't want his daughter to be up in no nigger house," the woman said.

I stopped, then turned around. I didn't understand what she meant. Why? Why wouldn't she want me in her house? I was bewildered. What did her words have to do with me?

That memory and the memory of Bernice holding my hand as we walked through the crowds when my father announced his candidacy for the governorship of sweet home Alabama are somehow forever tangled up like so many kudzu vines climbing up into the trees on the winding roads of the deep South.

THROUGHOUT THE DAYS that followed Daddy's announcement, Mama spent hours at the kitchen table writing letters and post-cards to addresses given to her by Wallace campaign volunteers who had gathered them at rallies or from distant relatives or the rolls of church memberships. It was done by hand, voter to voter—a laborious, painstaking outreach.

Daddy's first campaign for governor, 1958.

Wallace rallies were boisterous: gales of laughter from the antics of Minnie Pearl, twanging chords of steel guitars, young girls slapping tambourines against their thighs. Election officials and hometown notables paraded from one end of the platform to the other. Starstruck women with beehive hairdos clenched their hands beneath their double chins. "Dixie" blasted from car-mounted speakers. Daddy made his way through outstretched arms, strutting across the stage and saluting. This salute was one of his characteristic gestures, like his pointing finger stabbing upward. "How you doin', pardner?" he said, singling out people in the crowd, one hand in his coat pocket. He was cocky, snap-ping and strutting, a small, slight man with dynamic energy and tremendous charisma, the Confederacy's very own Napoleon. The Wallace campaign bounced from the Tennessee Valley to the Gulf of Mexico through the sultry spring. Daddy ripped the microphone from its stand. He quelled the crowds with the palm of his hand. They hung on his words. They sizzled with excitement.

POLITICAL PROGNOSTICATORS AGREED that the 1958 Democratic primary would not be won without a runoff. In 1958 and for four decades after, becoming the Democratic nominee was tantamount to winning the race. The November elections were only to make it official.

It's strange that perhaps more than any other single factor it was Daddy's opponent, John Patterson—a young, handsome lawyer from Phenix City, Alabama—who would shape our family's future and impact national politics and race relations. None of us could possibly have foreseen that.

Patterson seemed congenial but he was a racist in his heart. He had been thrust into the consciousness of the Alabama psyche when his father, Albert Patterson, was assassinated by local gangsters following his attempts to shut down their illegal gambling operations. Following his father's death, John took his place on the ballot and was elected. The loss of his father endeared John to the people of Alabama.

Although Daddy knew Albert Patterson, he was less familiar with his son, John. Patterson was not one of the movers and shakers, the Jefferson Davis Hotel lobby sitters who influenced Alabama politics. At first, Daddy was dismissive of Patterson: "All that kid has going for him is his dead father. That ain't enough to get him to the governor's office."

Daddy had yet to come to terms with the notion that Patterson's real appeal was his blatant racism. As the campaign began to tighten, and Patterson's racial rhetoric began to attract the Ku Klux Klan and white supremacists, Daddy scoffed at the notion and shrugged off suggestions that he needed to solidify his support with the Klan—which was especially active in the late 1950s in south Alabama, where the state's largest black population lived—by taking a position to the right of Patterson on the issue of integration.

Daddy continued to think that his best chance was to rail against income inequality and large corporations while promoting public education and promising roads, roads, and more roads. He targeted the concerns of the common man and headed to vote-rich north Alabama during the final weeks of the primary election, leaving Patterson to gin up the racists in the south.

Patterson and Daddy headed toward election day neck and neck. Daddy's pace was frenetic. His campaign workers and volunteers were pushed to the limit, and Mama joined him at rallies in North Alabama. He was on the verge of collapse: his voice was always hoarse and his suits hung slack on his gaunt frame. The only race he ever lost was as a college freshman when he bucked up against the college fraternities and ran for president of the Cotillion Club.

On June 3, Daddy came in second place: 162,435 votes, or 26 percent, to John Patterson's 196,859 votes, or 31 percent; the rest of the votes went to third-tier candidates. Daddy had three weeks to turn it around.

During the runoff, Patterson campaigned fiercely throughout the southern part of the state and continued to rely on racial rhetoric and his promises to keep Alabama white. He "was honored," he said, to be running with KKK support. He reminded white voters that as Alabama's attorney general, he obtained a restraining order to bar the NAACP from operating in Alabama on the grounds that it was not registered as an Alabama corporation. He made much of his suit against the Tuskegee Alabama Civic Association, a negro group that instigated an economic boycott in Tuskegee in protest of white attempts to gerrymander the town to protect white control. He did everything he could to remind the KKK and white voters that he was on their side.

ON THE MORNING of the runoff, my parents mingled with supporters on the courthouse steps in Clayton before going inside to vote. Daddy dropped Mama off at the house before heading to Montgomery. Mama fussed with her clothes as she packed her bags to travel to meet him. There was excitement in the house: a "we just know he is going to win" attitude prevailed. Mama's friends dropped by, sipped coffee at the kitchen table, and gave Mama fashion tips on what they thought a First Lady should wear. There were giddy discussions about what it would be like to live in such a grand place as the Alabama Governor's Mansion with cooks and handsome men in uniforms to drive Mama around.

When we arrived in Montgomery, the mood was festive. The air in the Greystone Hotel's ornate lobby was thick with cigar and cigarette smoke. Mama took us to our rooms. Daddy was with a small group of his campaign advisers, phoning county courthouses and campaign workers across the state.

"Peggy Sue, where are you?" Mamaw's sister, my aunt Bill, yelled out in her singsong way when she walked in our room. "I brought something special, just for you." She handed me a brown paper sack that was folded at the top. She looked over her shoulder at Mamaw. "I know I should've wrapped it, but I just slam ran out of time." I reached into the bag and pulled out a pair of pink plastic play high-heeled shoes. "Sugar," Aunt Bill said, "put those Cinderella shoes on and let's go downstairs and priss outside while your mama gets dressed."

I felt glamorous, although unsteady on my feet, as Aunt Bill and I walked along the downtown sidewalk. Aunt Bill pointed to one of the stores. "This is where your mama will take you shopping when your daddy wins."

We returned to the hotel and were waiting in a crowded suite when the first hint bloomed that Daddy could lose the election. As evening turned to night there was still hope that voting boxes in north Alabama would heavily favor Daddy and offset the lopsided numbers for Patterson coming from the state's southern counties. But as the night wore on, it became apparent that John Patterson would become the next governor. His hard-line racism had given him the edge. My father had lost.

———

DADDY GATHERED US up and took us to a waiting car to drive to a local television station on the outskirts of Montgomery. He was going to concede. I sat in the middle of the front seat next to Daddy and buried my face in his side. I felt his arm surround me as he pulled me close and whispered: "Well, we lost, sugah, but it is goin' to be all right. Sweetie, now don't you cry." The tears I was drying with the handkerchief he pulled from his pocket were not for me, they were for him.

While he was making his concession speech, we sat in the lobby to wait. Directly across from me there was a large wire cage, barren and rusting. Inside was a small monkey. I can still see it sixty years later. It looked as sad and lost and forlorn as I felt.

Following Daddy's televised remarks, we were driven back to the Greystone Hotel. A crowd of supporters, some crying, greeted him on the sidewalk as he stepped from the car. It was time for him to speak to his campaign supporters who were waiting for him. He was gracious in defeat. This is just the first round, he must have thought—I can hold on for four more years. He contained his anger and disappointment. My grandmother Mozelle's stoicism, her commitment to "never let anyone see you cry," had been passed down to my father.

Although there is disagreement about the events that immediately followed, depending on who tells the story, and overlooking Daddy's vague memory on the subject, it is generally agreed that Daddy said at some point that night, "I'll never be out-niggered again."

Those five words, spoken in the heat of his intemperance and rage, would follow us for the rest of our lives.

Later on in his life, Daddy told me several times that he had never said that. "Seymore Trammell, or somebody in his camp, just made that up. I would have never used the N-word like that."

Perhaps Daddy did not say those words on that night in 1958. But during his first term as governor, Daddy stood in the schoolhouse door, never punished or fired the state troopers that attacked marchers on the Edmund Pettus Bridge, and sent law enforcement officers to Birmingham to support Bull Connor's reign of terror in the summer of 1963.

6

Into the Darkness

*The most painful thing is losing yourself in the process of
loving someone too much and forgetting that you are
special too.*

—*Ernest Hemingway*

I f I had asked Daddy in the summer of 1958 if he was a racist,
I'm not sure what he would have said. For many years, I felt
obligated to defend Daddy's character and actions. I took the
official Wallace line: Daddy was a *segregationist* but not a racist.
Now I see that Daddy, in the words of Dan Carter, who wrote
The Politics of Rage, the definitive biography of my father and the
Wallace years, represented the reflexive racism of Southern men
and women of his generation.

What is the difference between a segregationist and a racist?
A racist is defined as a person who believes that one race is superior to others. To be a segregationist means upholding a caste

system—a system of apartheid. The idea of "separate but equal" was belied by the ways blacks were systemically terrorized with lynchings and beatings in the South (and the North too) and looked down upon and denied basic rights. There was nothing "equal" in segregation.

And yet, like so much in the South, it was complicated. I know in our house when I was growing up the use of the N-word was strictly forbidden. My parents would never have talked like that. But if I had asked Daddy after he lost the primary to Patterson in the summer of 1958 if he would do whatever it took to be elected governor in 1962, he would probably have said, "What do you think?" He would have done whatever it took to be elected.

OUR FAMILY LIFE was rough between Daddy's loss in '58 and his second run in '62. When Mama tried to console him after his loss to Patterson, he snapped back at her, was angry and often accusatory. When she broached the subject of "what is next in our lives," Daddy responded: "It's always on me to figure out a way to take care of you-all. When I tell you things will work out, that means *I* will figure it out."

The problem was that Daddy's track record of working things out was pretty dismal. Mama just gave up. "I guess we are all on our own," she must have thought to herself. She knew we were on the verge of sinking back into the kind of poverty that she had experienced before Daddy became a judge. Uncle Jack had taken over Daddy's circuit court judgeship and no more paychecks were coming. Mama took a part-time job at the Agricultural Extension Service in Clayton.

Daddy became a partner in Uncle Gerald's one-man law firm in Montgomery. On occasion he and Uncle Gerald would collect a fee from a client. Most of the time, Daddy was walking the streets, roustabouting with acquaintances and strangers. Money, in the form of "legal fees" from a few who believed that Daddy was going to win the next election and wanted to reserve a seat at the table, kept Daddy afloat in town.

Daddy's frequent absences from home continued. Montgomery, where Gerald had his office and where Daddy did his politicking, was two hours by car from Clayton. After his defeat, it often felt as if he had abandoned us. And on those days and nights when he did reappear at home, it usually was time to batten down the hatches. My parents' fights began in the general vicinity of the kitchen, roiled through the dining and living room, and often ended with the slam of their bedroom door. Their tumultuous confrontations were never physical, unless a flying ashtray or dinner plate hurled by Mama found its mark. Daddy's talent for the bob and weave of boxing no doubt worked to his advantage. My parents fought about money, my mother's sense of abandonment, or lipstick on his collar.

Mama had nothing of consequence with which to threaten Daddy.

"What can you do, Lurleen?" Daddy would say in a taunting voice. "You don't have any skills. You're not smart. Where are you going to go? How are you going to live?" He could be brutal. Hard as nails. I went numb inside when Daddy treated Mama this way. It was the only life I knew, and it was just the way my father was.

There never seemed to be a resolution—a coming together. Daddy wasn't satisfied until you came around to his point of view, no matter how long it took him to convince you. If Mama threw up her hands, turned, and walked away, Daddy would follow her or sit down beside her on the sofa. Daddy was through when he got through; Mama was going to listen.

As a young boy, Daddy watched as his daddy, usually drunk and in pain, raged through his house while his mother sat still in a chair. She never fought back, just waited for him to fall on the floor passed out, or move on out of the house, headed for some-place to drink and carouse. My father must have wanted his mother to strike back, to protect herself and the rest of them. But she never did. Daddy viewed not fighting back as a weakness. Mama's just giving up was not acceptable to him.

And yet Mama always believed that their marriage was worth saving. In spite of it all, she loved him.

DURING THAT PERIOD, Mama struggled to take care of us. I wore cardboard inside my shoes to cover the holes in the worn-out soles that winter. My grandparents sent what little money they could, and a seamstress friend of Mama's helped keep up our clothes. There was no talk in the house about our financial circumstances. Mama did what she had to do. She fed and clothed us.

Mama's meager circumstances were driven home to me years after she died. One of her friends who lived in Clayton when we did gave me a small cardboard box, the kind that a jewelry store would use for an expensive piece. Inside was an assortment of change and a little ledger sheet entitled CARD FUND. On the paper, Mama's name appeared along with the other members of the Friendly Card Club. The club collected monthly dues from its members to send cards to friends and families on special occasions. According to the ledger, all members of the card club had account credits by their names, except for Mama: she was a dollar and seventy-five cents in arrears.

GERALD AND DADDY'S Montgomery law office was a place frequented by more storytelling hacks and political wannabes than clients. But it was a crowd that Daddy could not pass up, as they offered opportunities for adulation that soothed Daddy's bruised ego after his trouncing by Patterson.

It also became the perfect place for Daddy to feel aggrieved. The people of Alabama had abandoned him (yet it never occurred to him that perhaps he himself had abandoned us). After many years of sobriety following his coming to terms with the effect alcohol had on him, Daddy began drinking again, and his anger and penchant for violence spiraled out of control.

On more than one occasion, Gerald was able to break up impending fistfights before the first punch was thrown. Daddy became indiscreet in his relationships with women, and the word soon spread through the grapevines of Montgomery society.

When Daddy was not holding forth in the law office, he could be found either in the lobbies and anterooms of one of the three hotels in downtown Montgomery or in the Elite Café. Although he no longer had a title to append to his name, most people still called him Judge. Some people thought it was beneath Daddy's dignity to chase down people in hotel lobbies or join an already occupied restaurant table and take over the conversation, but he did. He seemed desperate for attention. It was all he could do to keep up appearances with the little bit of money he was making from his law practice along with the paltry sums of cash slipped into his palm by still-faithful followers. In spite of the dire financial circumstances of our family, he showed no interest in getting a job.

DURING THE SPRING of 1959, Mr. Henry and Mamaw came for an extended visit and the house brightened. Mama and Mamaw sat in metal yard chairs in the backyard with cups of coffee and cigarettes and used Mr. Henry's slingshot to scare marauding mockingbirds feasting on ripening figs hanging from the limbs of the tree in our yard.

Mr. Henry carried his toolbox around the house looking for things that needed tending to. It was well known and a source of some amusement that Daddy was not one to have any interest or expertise on projects that required a nail, a hammer, or a screwdriver.

During their visit, Mamaw chose her words carefully on the issue of Mama's future. She quietly suggested coming back home with her and Mr. Henry. Mama could start over. It was no secret that the relationship between Mamaw and Daddy had always been less than perfect, but after the governor's race, Mamaw and Daddy's conversations became more heated and contemptuous when Daddy would occasionally come home from Montgomery.

With her back against the wall, Mama was faced with what she came to believe was the ultimate truth of her life. Her husband was drinking and womanizing in Montgomery and rarely home.

It was clear that what mattered to him was the adulation of the crowd and becoming governor of Alabama. His family was strictly secondary. She had no choice but to make her own way. And the thought of going home to the broken road must have felt as though she was taking refuge, returning to a place of safety and simplicity where she wouldn't have to wonder when and if my father was coming home and deal with his temper and his self-righteousness and self-serving sense of grievance—the fallout from his defeat.

She and Daddy had been married for sixteen years. She was thirty-three years old.

7

The Broken Road

We are all broken, that's how the light gets in.

—Ernest Hemingway

There is a photo of my mama, now lost in some obscure family album. She is sitting on the back porch steps of our house down in Clayton, her sleeveless white cotton blouse standing out against the black mesh of the screen door behind her. Her tanned legs are folded beneath her like the wings of a small bird. Elegant fingers drift through her coarse mane of chestnut hair. She holds a lit cigarette, tightly clenched in the fingers of her other hand. The frame focuses on her, but there are faint shadows of others. She looks beyond them with wistful resignation. Perhaps her solemnity and distant affect were the physical embodiment of her recognition that the life she hoped for would never come.

This photo might have been taken soon after she came back to live on the broken road. It was not even a road, just an abandoned roadbed, asphalt heaved up and cracked, mingling with kudzu and shrub trees along the side of a new and improved roadway. It was like a signpost of a first glance of happiness pointing to the way home, where moments of acceptance and love were always waiting.

My grandfather, Mr. Henry, used to tell Mama, he'd say, "Now Mutt, if things don't go to suit you down there with George and y'all need a place to stay, you come on up here and find the broken road cause we won't be far away."

Finding a place where life is safe, understandable and predictable, a no-time-to-pack-up-your-clothes car ride and, "yes, we have enough gas to get there," kind of place. Where "don't you be silly" and "that's ridiculous" sounds like laughter, rather than a hissing snake. Simple is better, not a place for complications, opening your eyes every morning when the sun comes through the window, warming up the room. Open doors to front porches, no need to lock the chain. Smiling because you want to, instead of smiling so they'll vote.

A life where contentment exists, with no secrets to keep or share, because there are none. No signposts needed, just look for the broken road. No longer a road to ride on, just there to point the way.

WHEN WE PASSED through Tuscaloosa, Alabama, to cross the bridge over the Back Warrior River, Mama always said, "Now you look for the broken road."

I stared out the window, looking hard to see. Then there it was, the abandoned road that would never abandon me. Can't ride it, can't walk it, just follow beside it to the end. Then you turn down that pig trail path, just wide enough to pass. And when you see that wooden house with flowers on the porch, roll down the window and wave your hands and happiness will wave you back.

Some of my happiest memories are of driving to the broken road with Mama.

A DIFFERENCE IN views among us, all based on the road we take. Back roads share secrets, tell stories, uncover the shame and the triumph of life, while the expressways just get you there, no cause for looking at all. No SEE ROCK CITY signs on barn tops, pulling off in a no-name town. Picking pears in an unfenced orchard. Scampering away to the tune of "who's out there stealing my pears."

My story is much like that of the broken road, heaved up and cracked for the truth of what power can do. It mingles amid history for the sake of the truth, gives rise to the inspiration that no matter who we belonged to "each of us can overcome," and offers hope that America will take the "road less traveled by" before it is too late.

The broken road of my childhood still remains with me, packed up somewhere inside, rustling around every now and then to remind me of those days in my life when everything was possible. Where Mr. Henry and my grandmother, Estelle Burns, sat on their front porch into the night. "Do you see any headlights?" Mamaw would ask. "Not yet," Mr. Henry would say. "Then look harder," she would reply.

No locked doors to bang on, no windows nailed shut. Perhaps one day, the broken road will call me home.

The lesson of the broken road is one of coming to terms with the past, not for the sake of forgetting or forgiving, but rather for truth. For history depends on what is told, taught, and accepted by those who lived it. The "we don't remember that the way you just said it, or that is not what I heard, or you should have been there" should encourage each of us to share and speak of what we saw, what we did and what others did for us and to us. For it is through our collective recollections that we, most often, will come closer to the truth. Saying "this just makes him, her, or those times back then look so bad" is no excuse.

The crossroads of history are littered with points of view, of the "how it was" rather than the "what it was," stark images in black and white. Much better to see them that way; all those blends and nuances of color and appliques of fabrics do nothing but get in the way. "We disagree" is certainly all right, but "why are you saying these things when it just looks so bad" is not.

No truth is ever complete, precision not required. But each of us should be willing to speak it as we know it, withdraw it when we just thought we knew it, and defend it when it can set a record straight, mend a broken heart, encourage acts of courage, and is the right thing to do. It's like Mr. Henry said one time: "The one that's yelling when you do the telling is the one who cooked the books."

MY HEART LIFTED at the sight of Mr. Henry and Mamaw's whitewashed wooden house with its rusting tin roof. It sat up on four brick pillars, just high enough for you to crawl underneath in case the cat had kittens next to the chimney rocks or some critter fell dead beneath the house and started smelling. The front porch sagged, but the tin roof did not leak when the rain fell, and the sound of pattering rain on it put you to sleep on rainy nights. In springtime, cleared-out spaces beneath pine trees and hardwoods were decked out with yellow daffodils and wild flowers. Dogwood trees and a few crepe myrtles were spread around the front yard.

The only modern conveniences at Mamaw and Mr. Henry's house were electricity and a telephone. Water was drawn from a

Mama with Mr. Henry, Mamaw, and her
older brother, Cecil Burns.

well not far from the back door of the house. A cast-iron pot hung from a homemade rusting iron swing-arm next to Mamaw's dugout fire pit. On washdays Mamaw used a beat-up boat oar to lift wet clothes from the boiling pot so she could hang them on the clothesline. If they happened to be bedsheets or homemade quilts, Mr. Henry had to stand up a notched board in the middle of the line to keep it from buckling. The outhouse, sitting just beyond a small garden plot behind the barn, was a one-holer. Bathing was done in privacy on the back porch with freshly drawn well water in a tin bucket and plenty of lye soap.

It wasn't easy to get from Clayton to Knoxville, Alabama. It was a long way along a series of two-lane blacktop roads. Mamaw and Mr. Henry's house was about sixty miles from the middle of the Mississippi state line, and Clayton was about eighty miles from the southwest corner of Georgia. We were like a pair of scissors cutting Alabama diagonally in half when we drove from our house to Mamaw and Mr. Henry's.

ON THE DAY we left for the broken road in the early summer of 1959, Daddy had not come home for several days. "Checking the pulse," he called his political moving around.

Mama was in a hurry. She didn't tell us we were going 'til the night before. She packed up what she could in suitcases and wedged the rest of our shoes and clothes and some cleaning supplies and jars of homemade preserves in cracks and crevices in the car.

"Here," she said, handing me a large bowl filled with figs. "Find some place to put them."

It was midafternoon before we left. "We're going to get caught by the dark before we get there," said Mama.

When Mama traveled without Daddy, she would look for a "rocking chair" to ride in—the space between two traveling eighteen-wheeler trucks. The first time I heard Mamaw tell Mama to ride in a rocking chair when she was driving alone or just with us, I asked Mamaw what that meant. "Well, it's like this," Mamaw said. "When your mama is driving on those blacktops through the woods and such, without your daddy (which is most of the time, I might add), she needs to get between two of those eighteen-wheelers so she can get some help if that worn-out junk car of hers breaks down. I would trust those truck drivers to help her before I would trust some man in a Cadillac."

I sensed my mama's spirit lighten as we left Clayton behind. Ashes from her cigarettes flew out of her rolled-down window as she drove. When we lost the radio signal out in the country-side, Mama would get us to sing with her, most times church songs.

> *How sweet and happy seem those days of which I dream,*
> *When memory recalls them now and then!*
> *And with what rapture my weary heart would beat.*
> *If I could hear my mother pray again.*
> *If I could hear my mother pray again,*
> *If I could hear her tender voice as then!*
> *So happy I would be,*
> *'Twould mean so much to me,*
> *If I could hear my mother pray again.*

As our car gained ground, climbing up hills and leaving the flat-lands of southeast Alabama behind, I never thought about asking Mama what our trip was about, how long were we going to stay or why we had left in such a hurry. A warm breeze blew through our rolled-down windows. My eyes were heavy. Just before I fell asleep I wondered what was going to happen when I let go of the bowl of figs I was still holding in my lap.

It was dark when Mama woke me.

"Where are we?"

"Almost to Tuscaloosa," Mama replied. Driving through the downtown, I asked her, "Is that the store where you worked when you met Daddy?"

"It's somewhere around here. Hold your breath," she said. The car climbed a small rise onto the bridge over the Black Warrior River. We passed through Northport and the highway narrowed. The broken road was close. A pale moon rose in the cloudless night, pushing itself up and over treetops and the red clay hills.

Then there it was, as always. The broken road.

MR. HENRY WAS nodding off in a chair on the front porch when we pulled up to the house. He always waited up when he knew we were coming. His strong arms felt good around me when he hugged me. We sat at the kitchen table with Mr. Henry while Mamaw stoked the fire to make a pot of coffee. Mamaw got a jar of milk out of the icebox and poured a glass and handed it to me. "Honey, your eyes look like you've been on a binge.

Drink this milk and let Mr. Henry go throw you in the bed. We can get all your clothes put out in the morning."

"I'll be there in a few minutes," Mama said.

The wallpaper in the room was light tan with bouquets of green-stemmed white lilies tied together with faint pink ribbons. An oscillating fan sat on the top of a small dresser; it blew the warmish air over us. The window curtains were pulled together with safety pins to keep the light out. Mama and I slept until the warming timbers in the attic began to pop.

Although it wasn't made clear to me in so many words, I could read between the lines. At first, this trip to Mamaw's felt no different from all the others. And then it did. My eyes were heavy, but I was happy when I sat down at the breakfast table. From what I was hearing, it sounded as though Mamaw and Mr. Henry were trying to persuade Mama to think about moving back up their way.

You would think I might have been dismayed at that prospect—but I wasn't. Instead, my spirits rose. At Mamaw and Mr. Henry's house there was no making a choice of whom to love or taking sides for one or the other. We all walked the same way. *Here comes a fork; let's all go this way. Wait a minute, I need to rest; then let's just sit right down, we can't go on without you.* There was never the sense of aimlessness and emptiness I felt in Clayton. "Honey, if you can't find something to do with yourself around this place, then you're not looking in the right places," Mamaw often said when we were visiting.

———

SEVERAL DAYS AFTER we arrived, I retreated to the front porch to escape the relentless heat that dragged moisture from the ground and hung it out to dry in suffocating layers of humidity. Mamaw was shelling butter beans.

"Go get you a pan. It's time to teach you how to shell butter beans without ripping your thumbnail off. See that darker green strip on the top? Take your little thumb and split it open, then wiggle it inside and push out the beans. Now it takes practice, honey. If you're not careful, that fingernail will pop off at the quick and you will be out of business, and I will have to soak that finger in alcohol. Here, swap pans with me. Let me go inside and get these washed up, then we'll have us a break."

I heard a car on the highway slow down and turn into our driveway. A dusty blue Ford emerged from beneath the crepe myrtle blooms. Mamaw watched from just inside the screen door as Uncle Gerald stepped out from behind the wheel and wished Mamaw a good morning.

"Nothing particular good about it as far as I can see," my grandmother replied. "What brings you to these parts?"

Without answering, he turned to me and with a quick grin said, "Come over here and give me a hug. You haven't gone off and married anybody, have you?'

A grudging smile crossed my face. "No, Uncle Gerald. I told you I would wait on you."

"Well, me and Buddy Holly both have a crush on Peggy Sue."

Mamaw stepped onto the porch. "Did you drive all the way up here from Montgomery this morning just to gab with us?"

"No, ma'am. I drove up last night and stayed in town. Got a late start this morning."

"Guess you had to push your company out the door this morning. Hope she was worth the money."

It was obvious that Mamaw was ready for a showdown. "Peggy Sue, go find Henry and tell him your uncle Gerald has just showed up."

I ran back behind the house where Mr. Henry was tending to his elderly plow mule, Bertis. "Now that Bertis has a new pair of shoes, what say we let her take you on a ride around the pen. You, me, and Bertis need to get to plowing this field. Time to plant is comin'."

After I told him Uncle Gerald was up front, all thoughts of riding or plowing were put aside. Mr. Henry pulled a handkerchief from his rear overall pocket and wiped his face and the two of us headed toward the front of the house, him moving along with a giddy-up walk, an uneven and awkward gait with a hitch in each step, and me right behind him.

After we rounded the corner of the house, Mr. Henry confronted Uncle Gerald head-on. "She's not going back this time, Gerald. She is where she belongs, and we are going to take care of her until she can get back on her feet."

Mamaw looked at me. "Sugar, you just cover up those ears."

"She shoulda cracked a cola bottle over your brother's head a long time ago," Mamaw said.

"I hear you, Mrs. Burns," Uncle Gerald replied. "But George has big plans. He's running for governor again. You know he never really stopped after he got beat. And what kind of life will Lurleen have living with you up here in the country? I can't promise George will ever change, but he can give Lurleen things she never dreamed of and take her places she has never been."

"How can she expect him to do that when he can't take his fine self up here himself to talk to Lurleen?"

"George figured Lurleen will likely listen to me before anyone else."

"Lurleen will never have any peace of mind living with him," Mr. Henry said.

Uncle Gerald didn't take him up on that. Perhaps he knew it was true. Instead, he looked my way. "I bet your mama has gone fishing. Let's go find her."

WE PICKED UP a pig trail behind the barn and walked toward a creek, not far from Mr. Henry's back property line. Mama, with her back facing us, was sitting beneath a mimosa tree on a flipped-over wooden crate that had seen its better days. A cane pole was propped up in a crook of one of the tree's branches. Mama's chin rested on her pulled-up knees, her eyes following a white ball cork drifting in one of the creek's washouts.

The creek was a spring-fed tributary of the Black Warrior River. Mama never called it anything other than "the creek down behind the house." It was mostly narrow with high red clay banks. When the creek was running high in the late winter and spring, the fast-moving water would carve out washouts in some of the creek's curves. When the low water came in the summer, the washouts were where the fish were.

"Why, look who's here," Gerald said in his most pleasant voice.

Mama opened her metal tackle box and pulled out a crumpled pack of Camel cigarettes and passed one to Gerald. She uncrossed her legs and stood up. "I expected you to show up at some point."

Uncle Gerald looked down at me. "Why don't you run on back to the house while I talk to your mama for a minute."

Some years after Mama died, I asked Uncle Gerald about their conversation on that day.

"Daddy says you two ganged up on him," I said.

"Me and your mama ganged up on him a lot of times," he replied. "As long as we let your daddy think he was winning, even when he wasn't, he would wave his cigar around like it was some voodoo stick and tell us: 'You two think you can outsmart me, but you can't!' We'd thank him for listening, let the dust settle, then do what we needed to do anyway.

"When Lurleen took you up to Knoxville, at first I don't think your daddy even knew you were gone! It probably took him a few days to wonder why all of your clothes went missing. When 'I think she left me!' dawned on him, I bet he almost fainted, got mad, stomped around the house and then called me.

"'Go up there and talk some sense into her,' he said.

"So your daddy sent me up there to bring all you home." Gerald said. "Your mama and I had a rough conversation on that creek bank after she sent you back to the house. She was mad as hell and told me she had had enough of your daddy and the way he ignored all of you. And of course everything she said was the God's truth. I had no argument for any of her very valid complaints.

"I told your mama that your daddy loved her, and I believed she loved him. We all knew he was most times an SOB, so that was not something I could get around. But I told her that after all the crap she had been through, if she could just stay around a little bit longer, she could be First Lady of Alabama. And you children would be able to live in the Governor's Mansion and have a kind of life that most people only dream of. This is Gerald you're talking to, I told her. I know better than most what you have been through with George. I wish things were different but both of us know that he is not going to change. He loves you, you know that, but he just doesn't know how to show it.

"Your mama said that if your daddy loved her, he needed to learn fast how to act like he loved her. And I agreed. What could I say? I think she called him a penny-pinching skinflint, which of course he still is.

"'Even if he had money, he wouldn't even know how to write a check,' your mama said." We both laughed at that one.

"Mama must have been on a roll when y'all talked," I said. "I should have stayed at the creek with you!"

"Your mama said she would call your daddy that night. I told your daddy he had better be listening out. Well, you know what happened. She called him a bunch of times and he either was not at the house or didn't pick up the phone, but I damn well know he knew she was going to call him 'cause I told him she was. After that, the shit didn't just hit the fan, it knocked it over!"

I REMEMBER MAMA trying to call Daddy several times the day after Uncle Gerald came for a visit. She asked the operators to double-check the number. Finally, she gave up. Mamaw and Mama mostly sat out on the porch the rest of the day.

"I'm too tired to fix a big supper. Just eat what we got." I remember Mamaw saying that, because a pot of something was always boiling on the stove when we were there.

The next morning, I woke up to a singing Mamaw and the smell of bacon in the air.

"Your Mama had to run over to Eutaw this morning. She has some business at the courthouse. Should be back way before dark."

Mamaw brought me a plate piled high with breakfast food. "Y'all all need to go ahead and finish this up so I can put on supper and get around to at least one batch of fried apple pies."

THE GREENE COUNTY courthouse, a rather dour building, stood amid scattered stores and small offices in downtown Eutaw, Alabama.

Mama sat down across the desk from a young lawyer who asked what he could do for her.

"I want a divorce," Mama said.

"Name and occupation of your husband?" the lawyer asked.

"George Wallace, and he is unemployed at the moment." Mama always laughed at that part of her story. "You should have seen that lawyer's face."

"Did you say George Wallace?"

"That's what I said."

"The same George Wallace that was the judge and just ran for governor?"

"One and the same."

"What grounds?"

"You name it, he's probably done it!" That was what Mama claimed she said.

Mama told the lawyer she wanted him to get it filed as fast as he could.

MAMA TOLD MAMAW the details of her courthouse trip while we were sitting on the front porch that night. Mamaw said something like, "Are you sure you are doing the right thing?"

It seemed at one point Mamaw started backing up, asking Mama if she was sure about divorcing Daddy. She said something to the effect of, "This is a big decision, no matter how I feel about George." (I think she actually called him "a little scoundrel.") "If he's still in the picture at least there would be some money coming in to make your bills each month."

"Well, how has that been going for me these past sixteen years?" Mama told Mamaw that while she might not have been the most important person in Daddy's life, she was the most powerful.

"Have you ever heard of a divorced man being elected governor of Alabama? Or better yet, have you ever heard of a divorced man with a bunch of children running around missing their daddy being elected governor?" Mama said.

"Can't say as I have."

"Well, neither have I. George tells me and everybody else who will listen that next time around he's going to win and be governor of Alabama. No ifs, ands, or buts. Strutting around. The one thing he can't lose is me. I just hate that it took me this long to figure this out. He needs me more that I need him, and things are going to change."

My grandmother looked at her daughter with pride. "All hell is about to break loose," she said.

"I bet we are going to have a visitor in a couple of days," Mama said, and I knew she was talking about Daddy.

When my daddy did get the news that Mama had filed for divorce, Gerald told him that they were driving up to the broken road. "If you ever want to be governor, you have to make up with Lurleen and start acting right. I told you to never underestimate her."

"Well, what if she won't listen?" Daddy said.

"Then you will be a two-time loser and going to somebody else's inauguration come January of 1963."

WHEN MAMA SAW Daddy pull up in the driveway in Uncle Gerald's car, she told me to go give him a hug. Mamaw was peeking from around her bedroom door. I squealed as Daddy picked me up and raised me over his head. "How's my Uudlum Scuudlum?" He pulled out a bag of M&M's from his right coat pocket and handed it to me. "I sure do miss you. Our house gets mighty lonely when you are not around."

"Have you come to take us home?" I asked.

"That's what I wanted to talk to your mama about. Why don't you go find her for me?"

I remember seeing Daddy and Mama standing in the front yard. Daddy paced around; Mama leaned up against the car, hands folded across her chest. It seemed to me they were somewhere in between a hug and a fight.

Sometime after the sun went down but before the moon came up, Mama and Daddy came up into the house.

"You're gonna stay up here with Mamaw and Henry for a while," Daddy told me. "Your mama and I have some things to work out."

Daddy and Mama kissed me goodbye, and then they left. I didn't feel abandoned. I loved my grandparents and felt at home on the broken road.

I STAYED BY the broken road for the rest of that summer. In the fall, I went to school in Eutaw. Mr. Henry drove the school bus. "First one on, first one off," he would say.

In November, I caught the measles. Mamaw warmed water from the well on her wood-fired stove, poured it into a large metal washtub sitting on the kitchen floor, and bathed me to bring my fever down.

There were times when I missed Mama and Daddy. But the simplicity and ease of living with my grandparents felt magical to me. The house was calm and quiet and peaceful. Sometimes on the weekends we would ride over to Tuscaloosa to visit relatives. One day we went to the picture show.

About a week or so before Christmas, Mama and Daddy came back; they had reconciled. We all waved back to Mamaw and Mr. Henry as we drove away. "They'll be visiting us soon," Mama said.

While we were stopped at the end of Mr. Henry's driveway to let a car go by, I said, "Daddy, now you help me find the broken road."

Daddy looked briefly at me over his shoulder. "Not this time, sugah. We're goin' a different way."

8

You Got What You Wanted

Politics is a matter of choices, and a man doesn't set up the choices himself. And there is always a price to make a choice. You know that. You've made a choice, and you know how much it cost you. There is always a price.

—*Robert Penn Warren*

I n December 1959, we were back in Clayton. Daddy slept through Christmas morning as usual while Mama handed out the gifts and offered cheerful commentary. Things had improved between them. During the early months of 1960, Daddy's homecomings were more frequent and congenial than had been customary. On Friday nights, Daddy and I had a standing date to watch the boxing matches on TV. We picked a favorite in each bout and cheered for our man as if we were in the arena ourselves. We high-fived and ate M&M's. Daddy would often jump to his feet during heavy action, prowling around the den like a boxer himself, stabbing the air with his fists. He was ferocious and inflamed. And then he'd plop down next to me with fierce hugs, tousling my hair. He could be rough; sometimes I had to tell him to stop, although I relished his affection and attention and wouldn't have traded it for anything in the world.

I found myself living on the verge of happiness. His relationship with Mama ebbed and flowed, as it always had. There were times when he brooded, looking out to the street from behind the living room curtains as if he was expecting someone to come by and save him from claustrophobic domesticity, to whisk him away to where the action was—Montgomery, the capital.

He was preparing for his next run for governor against the backdrop of Alabama and broadly Southern politics and also what was happening nationally. After his loss to John Patterson, Daddy faced the moral quandary of whether to continue his moderate position on the issue of race or take a hard turn to the right. In 1960, the U.S. Supreme Court ruled that segregated waiting rooms, lunch counters, and restrooms used by interstate travelers were unconstitutional. The following year the Congress of Racial Equality (CORE) organized interracial groups to ride on interstate buses throughout the South to test whether President Kennedy and Attorney General Robert Kennedy would enforce the law.

On May 13, 1961, Dr. Martin Luther King Jr. and others expressed their concerns about traveling into Alabama. It was rumored that the KKK would launch attacks. Their warnings were unheeded. One of the buses was firebombed on the outskirts of Anniston, Alabama; in Birmingham, the elected public safety commissioner Bull Connor agreed to give the Klan a head start to attack the bus at the station before he would show up. The Klan did just that.

A week later, Freedom Riders boarded a bus to Montgomery. In light of the attacks in Anniston and Birmingham, President Kennedy secured a commitment from Governor Patterson that the bus would be protected. Patterson provided escorts for the bus from Birmingham to the Montgomery city limits, but not to the bus station itself.

When the bus arrived at the station, a mob of more than two hundred people was waiting. The riders who could not escape were severely beaten, as were news reporters, cameramen, and photographers. The Justice Department observer John Seigenthaler was beaten with a tire iron and left on the street as ambulances refused to take him and others to local hospitals—because they were black, and those whites, "they were nothing but agitators."

Governor Patterson, who had supported President Kennedy in his presidential race, refused to speak to the president when he called. Several days later four hundred U.S. marshals were sent to Montgomery to maintain the peace. Patterson publicly objected and told them to go home and threatened them with arrest if they broke the law.

The following day, fifteen hundred African Americans gathered at Ralph Abernathy's First Baptist Church in downtown Montgomery to pray. That night more than fifteen hundred whites surrounded the church and threatened the U.S. marshals. President Kennedy forced Patterson to call out the National Guard and declare martial law. Patterson continued to denounce the Freedom Riders.

Patterson's popularity soared among whites with each beating, burning, arrest, and humiliation of African American men, women, and children. Governor Patterson's refusal to speak to

President Kennedy when Kennedy attempted to seek his advice on the situation was seen as a victory for the South; to some, it was seen as even more so than Robert E. Lee's victory in the Battle of Chancellorsville during the Civil War.

On June 2, 1961, *Time* magazine's cover story featured Alabama and the Freedom Riders, including a cover photograph of Governor Patterson standing in front of the Confederate monument on the Alabama capitol grounds. A white carnation was pinned to the left lapel of his suit coat. While the carnation seemed innocuous, the Alabama KKK, officially named the Knights of the White Carnation, got the message loud and clear. Governor Patterson became a hero to middle-class whites, reminding Alabamians that "integration will come over my dead body."

DADDY WATCHED ALL this, calculating. And then, in December 1961, Daddy prepared to run. With the Christmas tree still standing in the corner of our living room, our lives changed and we abruptly left Clayton for the last time. My baby sister Lee was eight months old. There were no hugs and kisses from neighbors, no going-away gifts or parties; my school friends and I had no time to say goodbye. We packed our clothes, turned off the lights, and locked the kitchen door behind us. I didn't know what was happening. To me this was just another road trip, and I regret that now. Our home on Eufaula Street was full of the things that could have brought memories back from my childhood to share with my children. That whole part of my life would disappear as if it never happened, and I had no inkling of what lay ahead.

Daddy had promised Mama that he would be with her—and uprooting us was the price. He needed to be in the capital to effectively launch his campaign.

We moved into a low-rent apartment complex in Montgomery, on the edge of the wrong side of town, with a broken asphalt parking lot, scrawny boxwood bushes, mostly dead, and patches of red dirt. We had a compact living room with dark wood paneling, a breakfast nook and a closet under the stairs, a cramped kitchen behind a swinging door, one small bathroom with cracked tiles, and two small bedrooms. The furniture was a collection of hand-me-downs; our dinner plates and glasses were mismatched.

During the first six months of 1962, we barely had enough to eat. Sometimes Mama brought food home from Wallace rallies. She walked to a small grocery store some three blocks away and bought what she could on credit to get us through.

Perhaps Mama knew what she was getting into, and she was willing to pay the price to be with Daddy. As for me, I wondered if moving to Montgomery so that I could be closer to Daddy was worth the effort, but it was not my decision. I suspected that my days of boxing match marathons and M&M's were over.

FOLLOWING THE CHRISTMAS break, Mama took me to enroll at Bellingrath Junior High School. Most of the students came from the surrounding middle-class neighborhoods where modest to large ranch houses with low-slung roofs perched on manicured lawns. I walked the four or five blocks from the apartment to school. Girls stood in hallways and looked at me as I walked by. Curious stares sometimes turned into mocking eyes. "Those country clothes," I heard one girl say.

Not long after I enrolled, I was cited by a crossing guard for inadvertently jaywalking. The citation was sent from the principal's office to my teacher Clara McQueen. Upon receipt, Miss McQueen sent me to the principal's office on a feigned mission of some sort. During my absence, she informed my classmates that I was going to be a part of Alabama's First Family following Daddy's election as governor, and I was to be treated as such, and under no circumstances was I ever to be cited again by any student crossing guard. Although Miss McQueen's lecture did little to endear me to my fellow students, it made me realize that my life as a Wallace meant something to others and proved to me that I finally had someone on my side.

Miss McQueen became an important part of my life. She noticed that I could not read the writing on the chalkboard even from the first row. Each day, she allowed me to stay after school so that I could stand close to the board and copy the assignments for the next day. She called Mama to suggest that I needed glasses. Mama was both polite and appreciative and no doubt embarrassed when she asked Miss McQueen to allow me to continue staying after school until she could get the money from Daddy for a pair of glasses. Following their conversation, my after-school stays lasted for several more weeks.

BY MAY 1962, the second Wallace campaign for governor was in full swing. Daddy's every moment was filled with his determination to win. He was frenzied and focused; he saw this as his last shot at fulfilling his boyhood dream.

Of the nine Democratic candidates on the ballot, there were only three stalking horses, one of which was Daddy. The campaign was brutal, with Daddy constantly on the move, endlessly driving around the state, staying in the cheapest hotels, shaking thousands upon thousands of hands deep into the night.

Here is when Daddy's vow never to be "out-niggered again" came fully into play. Supporters roared with approval at his coded talk of segregation and white supremacy. At a rally in Montgomery on March 10, Daddy stood before a packed crowd and pledged that he would "stand in the schoolhouse door," personally, with his own body, to "block the integration of Alabama schools." He would stand up for states' rights. He would not allow the federal government to interfere with the customs and mores of Southern life. He promised the Confederacy all over again. In some ways, with his viciousness and negativity, Daddy defined and crystalized what has become the tenor of modern political life. He described his old friend and new nemesis Judge Frank Johnson, in Johnson's own hometown, as an "integrating, carpetbagging, scalawagging, race-mixing, bald-faced liar." The crowd roared. At a north Alabama rally, he proclaimed: "I will continue to fight for segregation in Alabama because it is based on our firm conviction of right, and because it serves the best interests of all our people . . . We shall fight the federals in the arena of an increasingly sympathetic national public opinion . . . I pledge to stand between you and those who would impose on you doctrines foreign to our way of life and disruptive of the peace and tranquility of our citizens. I will face our enemies face to face, hip to hip and toe to toe and never surrender the governor's office to these modern-day carpetbaggers, scalawags, and polliwogs. Right will prevail if we fight."

Perhaps most hurtful to me as I look back is that the Klan was on board for Daddy's run—and he was glad to have them. Thunderous crowds gathered all across the state to hear Daddy speak while volunteers, including Klan members, worked the crowd—the same Klansmen who were against Daddy in 1958. "George Wallace is on our side this time," KKK members would proudly say.

Was Daddy's decision just about the price of admission to win the governor's race, or did he believe in what the KKK stood for? Did it really matter? Either way, it was the only way Daddy could win.

Mattered to him? Maybe not. Mattered to our family? He never asked.

DADDY LED THE Democratic Party primary contest but was forced into a runoff, which he won on June 24, 1962, sealing his victory. The general election in November would be nothing but going through the motions.

On the night of the runoff, we stood on the stage at the Jefferson Davis Hotel. Daddy grabbed my hand and said, "Sugah, we won! We won!" Mama waved at the crowd. Mamaw and Mr. Henry stood on one side of the auditorium. Mr. Henry wiped his eyes with his handkerchief. Uncle Gerald worked the crowd, all squeezed together and cheering. Mama's happiness was contagious: no more worries about food to eat, or mending clothes late into the night. We were going to live in a mansion with a bedroom for each of us.

Daddy waded into the crowd of excited supporters who had worked tirelessly for him. "Not like the last party we had four years ago," he said. I heard a supporter say, "Now we're the ones on top."

Mama's excitement, or just relief, was evident as she smiled and hugged all of us and then her friends. Even Mamaw managed a grin. Aunt Bill pulled out a Kleenex from her pocketbook and wiped her eyes. "Peggy Sue, you just come over here and give your Aunt Bill a big old hug," she said.

HAVING A FATHER who is adulated by boisterous crowds and lusted after by women sitting beneath oversized hair dryers in small-town beauty parlors because he stomped on the inherent rights of people he was supposed to be serving makes for a rather clouded conscience for a questioning daughter who sees the truth going a-kilter. Such was the struggle of my life in the beginning of the Wallace reign in Alabama.

My parents were suddenly celebrities. Their star power drew crowds at football games, rodeos, barbecues, and even simple outings at local meat-and-threes (restaurants serving a meat entrée with three sides). It was exciting to see menus, football programs, and Dairy Queen napkins thrust into Daddy's hands for his almost unintelligible signature. But I was also aware of the snatches of racists' conversations that accompanied all the hoopla:

"Governor, I gotta thank you for keeping them in their place, my whole family voted for you." "We gonna hold you to your promises to keep them out of our schools."

In late June 1962, we moved to an elegant rental house that was more appropriate for a First-Family-in-waiting. Mama shopped for our inauguration clothes. It was an exciting time—a summer of great expectations, no worries about our tomorrows.

Although Montgomery blue bloods shied away from our countrified family, most people in Alabama breathed sighs of relief following Daddy's election. With Wallace in the governor's office, they could put all that talk about integration behind them.

Though Daddy's predecessor, John Patterson, had talked a good game about segregation and had no problem brutalizing African Americans, he was not George Wallace, and now things were really going to change. "Because George is one of us, he came up the hard way. You know he was a boxer and a scrabbler. You can't hear him and not believe it's the God's truth. He's gonna make 'em stop, look, and listen!" Daddy was anointed, and white folks began to whistle "Dixie" again.

On Christmas morning, Mama gave me a beautiful knee-length plaid wool coat, adorned with large buttons down the front, to wear on Daddy's inauguration day.

9

The Victory Is Ours

We all live in a house on fire, no fire department to call,
no way out, just the upstairs window to look out of while
the fire burns the house down with us in it.

—Tennessee Williams

On Saturday, January 12, 1963, two limousines stood parked, their engines running, in front of our temporary home on Thomas Avenue in the fashionable part of Montgomery. We were going for dinner at our new home, the Alabama Governor's Mansion, built in 1907 as the private residence of Robert Ligon Jr., a statesman and attorney. In 1950, then governor Jim Folsom bought the house to serve as the residence of Alabama's First Families. Its graceful neoclassical style befitted an official residence of governors. During the time Mama and Daddy served in office, it would become known as "the People's Mansion."

The limousines, accompanied by a state trooper escort, lights flashing, drove slowly through the streets of Montgomery before passing through the gates of the mansion on South Perry Street. Floodlights lit the white facade and stately columns. I was filled with wonder. The staff of butlers and maids stood on either side to greet us. "Welcome to your new home," said one of the butlers. He opened the pair of mahogany front doors, and we stepped inside.

A glittering crystal chandelier lit the entryway in front of a grand staircase carpeted in red and curving back on itself on either side. On the wall of the first landing, a portrait of Daddy had already been hung. Our awestruck eyes took in all the magnificence. With great excitement in her voice, Mama said, "Just think, you can have all you want to eat at any time. All you need to do is ask." Many years later, reflecting on that moment with Mama, I wondered if it was her way of apologizing to us for the many nights we had gone to bed hungry.

After touring the mansion's downstairs, we were led up a back staircase to our living quarters. The bedrooms with private baths were large, with dark wood furnishings and heavy drapes. In the center of the two wings, a large sitting room overlooked the main entrance hall.

We went back downstairs and sat at a table with fine china and sterling silver, where we were served a dinner of steak with baked potatoes and salads. Beside Daddy's plate was a large bottle of ketchup. The staff had been forewarned that Daddy put ketchup on all his food and preferred to shake it from a bottle rather than spoon it from a china bowl.

The following day, the Thomas Avenue house was chaotic as friends and relatives stopped by. My two grandmothers exchanged frosty greetings before separating, Mozelle to the living room and Mamaw to the kitchen.

Mozelle was proud of her son's accomplishments, but she didn't congratulate Mama for her hard work and sacrifice as well. Even at such a time, Mozelle was stoic and withdrawn. She never warmed up to Mama in spite of Mama's many attempts to make her a part of our family.

Mama was both excited and apprehensive. The next day she was going to become Alabama's First Lady. A small-town girl, somewhat shy and withdrawn, who liked nothing better than sitting on the bank of a river watching a floating cork bob up and down, she was about to step into the pages of history.

THAT AFTERNOON DADDY's friend Seymore Trammell came by the house and picked him up to head downtown and put the final touches on his inaugural speech. Although Seymore and Daddy had been close during the time they worked together in the circuit court when Seymore was a district attorney and Daddy was a judge, Seymore's racism had driven him into the Patterson camp in the 1958 governor's race.

When Daddy decided to embrace segregation and hit hard on it in every speech he made in his second statewide run, Seymore could not have been more pleased. After all, he and Daddy had been partners in crime long before that, as I would learn quite by chance.

It seemed that during the six years that Daddy and Seymore rode the circuit, they would stay together in Midway, Alabama, a small country community halfway between the courthouses of Union Springs and Clayton. I found out about this when, many years later, my husband, Mark, my son Burns, and I went to our church to have our photo taken for the church directory. We were introduced to a middle-aged woman sitting behind the photographer's table who I could tell recognized my name.

"You look just like your dear mother," she said. "It's in the eyes and that thick hair of yours."

"Well, thank you very much," I said.

"You know, I grew up in Midway. When your daddy was a judge we would see him and Mr. Seymore Trammell. My daddy said it just made sense when the two of them stayed in that house in Midway just down the road from where we lived to cut that long drive in half. They were both real nice men."

"We never had a house in Midway," I responded. "Our house was in Clayton."

Still smiling, she replied, "Well, of course you did! You did have a house in Midway because your daddy lived there on and off."

"And I know we did not have a house in Midway," I said in an rising voice.

The woman leaned forward and squinted. She knew she was right and not even a daughter of George Wallace was going to accuse her of lying, especially in a church.

Before I could reply, Mark spoke up. "You know, I think I did hear about that. They're ready for us, Peggy."

As we were being adjusted on a seat for the photograph, Burns leaned in and whispered to Mark, "Poor Mom."

THROUGHOUT HIS MANY years of service to Daddy, Seymore Trammell presented himself as a man of gallantry and gentility.

Seymore was short with freckles on his face that matched his thick red hair. His speech was precise with a hint of mint julep thrown in. His immaculate dress, with shined-up shoes and the gold chain of a pocket watch tethered to his pants, was at times hard to swallow, particularly when his racist views reared their ugly heads.

Seymore Trammell had said to others that he was going to make sure that Daddy was not out-niggered again. Toward that end, he convinced Daddy that Asa Carter, from the northwest Alabama city of Oxford, was the perfect person to help him with his inaugural speech. Carter was involved with the KKK. He was waiting in the small downtown office when Daddy and Seymore arrived the day before the inauguration. Daddy's inaugural speech was laying on the desk. Carter picked it up and began flipping through the pages. "Here it is, on the fifth page." He said as he handed the speech to Daddy. "This is the most important part." It read, "In the name of the greatest people that have ever trod this earth, I draw the line in the dust and toss the gauntlet before the feet of tyranny and I say segregation now, segregation tomorrow, and segregation forever."

Wallace loyalists noted that Daddy's speeches during his 1962 campaign had taken on a malevolent tone, more about segregation and less about progress. Only a few were aware that the new and revised language of George Wallace was from the pen of Asa Carter, one of the most virulent racists in Alabama, a thug and a criminal with a reputation for murderous violence. Perhaps Daddy thought he could backtrack once victory was his, which is a much easier pill for me to swallow—though I know it shouldn't be—as I wonder, even today, if he really meant what he said.

JANUARY 14, 1963, Daddy's inauguration day, was very cold, 28 degrees with a wind chill of zero. That didn't deter the great sea of people who had gathered. They came from all walks of life—factory workers, farmers, bankers, preachers. No one thought about sitting it out. George Wallace was "just folks like us," and he was going to take out after the cheaters and the liars that made the money while common folk couldn't cover their bills each month. But even more important, he was going to show the blacks just how white folks felt about them and bring back law and order the way it should be. Sometimes things might get real bad for a white man: no job, no money, and a daughter pregnant at fourteen by a no-count. But in the minds of many who gathered, there was one thing to be thankful for. They were not black.

Daddy stood, as had other governors before him, on the brass star that denoted the very place where Jefferson Davis stood on the front portico of the capitol when he took his oath of office as president of the Confederate States of America. Behind him, on the second floor of the white capitol building itself, was the chamber where the Confederate States of America was formed. Catty-corner across the street was the first "White House of the Confederacy," the house that Davis had lived in. With his hand on the Bible that had been used at Davis's inauguration, Daddy was sworn in as Alabama's forty-fifth governor. He faced the broad expanse of downtown Montgomery's main boulevard,

Dexter Avenue, that ran to Market Square, the place where African men, women, and children had been sold into slavery.

A military band played as we descended the capitol steps and walked up onto the reviewing stand where Daddy would speak. The crowd was expectant and hopeful that he would rouse in their hearts a sense of pride in their Alabama, the Alabama that for generations had been given short shrift by the rich, powerful, blue-nosed sophisticates in the North.

We sat on either side of the podium huddled together under electric blankets to ward off the cold. The crowd standing behind Daddy seemed restless, many dressed in work clothes and jackets rather than their Sunday best, loyalists who would fight for him at the drop of a hat. But they seemed out of place now, standing behind Alabama's new governor, who was dressed in a long-tail morning coat and ascot with a top hat at his feet.

The inaugural parade lasted five hours and was a grand affair with bands and floats from all of Alabama's sixty-seven counties and white colleges and universities. It particularly pains me to report that the inaugural parade committee, at Daddy's direction, banned all African American schools and colleges from participating, including the Tuskegee Institute, on whose board of trustees he served.

That night, a lavish inaugural ball was held at Garrett Coliseum. Spotlights high on the top of the building lit the winter night. Inside, men in tuxedos and women in formal dresses grumbled when they were served punch or hot coffee rather than champagne. The stands filled up with Wallace people. They had come without invitation to watch their George and that sweet Lurleen dance the first dance.

The coliseum floor was suddenly cast into darkness. A booming voice came over the speakers as an orchestra began playing "Stars Fell on Alabama": "Ladies and gentlemen, Governor George Corley Wallace and First Lady Lurleen Burns Wallace." My parents were bathed in brilliant white light. The crowd roared as they slowly pivoted together, Daddy saluting and Mama waving her gloved hand. The gold-and-yellow brocade of Mama's dress complemented her bare tanned shoulders, pearl necklace, and long white kid gloves. I wore a floor-length gown of silver metallic brocade and kid gloves. Daddy looked debonair in his cutaway tuxedo. "Sugah, are you happy?" Daddy asked as the orchestra began to play and he took my hand to dance. "Watch your step," he said. Mama danced with my younger brother, George Jr.

It was late when we were driven back through the gates of the Governor's Mansion. Still in my long dress, I wandered through the first-floor rooms. Low light cast shadows on the portraits in the First Lady's Room; the dining room chandelier was lit. In the long rectangular sitting room, a pair of floor-to-ceiling pier mirrors stood directly across from each other. As I stood between them my reflection fell back on itself again and again. I was fractured but whole; a carefree life was now mine. No sadness could come calling in such a magical place. My thirteenth birthday was just two weeks away.

10

1963

I was a citizen of Birmingham close to the age of the girls who died in the bombing. But I was growing up on the wrong side of the revolution.

—*Diane McWhorter*

D addy never trusted more than a handful of people, and at times he was willing to look the other way when close friends or allies did mischief in his name. But back him into a corner or embarrass him, whether in fun or intentionally, and you were doomed. He had an unnerving penchant for remembering the slightest insult, whiff of disloyalty, or even hint that you thought you were smarter than he was. That applied not only to the public but to our family as well.

But Daddy also had an aversion to throwing hatchets at people in his inner circle who did things that did not meet with his approval, which meant that he had to have others close by who would do that for him. Al Lingo was Daddy's hatchet man. His trademark oversized black plastic-framed glasses gave him a comical but sinister look. He was thick-bodied, with large hands and short legs. In public, he was never seen without a hat. He carried a sidearm and a billy club much as a businessman would carry a briefcase and pocket watch.

Lingo was born in my childhood hometown of Clayton but grew up in Eufaula, where I was born. He owned his own plane and flew Daddy to various political events in 1958. He was a strong supporter of Daddy's in the 1962 election. He was an outsider, a devout racist, and a man's man, tough, with a temper, ready to fight. Although Lingo had no law enforcement training or work experience (he was a cabinet manufacturer), Daddy announced soon after his election that Lingo would be appointed to the position of director of public safety and would thereafter be known as Colonel Al Lingo.

Daddy took pride in his belief that he was good at reading people, judging their character. To many, his appointment of Lingo would prove to be one of the biggest mistakes he ever made. Perhaps he felt obligated to show the people of Alabama that when he said, "Segregation now, segregation tomorrow, and segregation forever," he really meant it.

WITHIN WEEKS OF his appointment, Lingo renamed the Alabama Highway Patrol the Alabama State Troopers, refitted their uniforms, and issued them steel helmets and short-barrel carbines, a shoulder-fired rifle with a barrel length of less than sixteen inches, a firearm for the military but not for a law enforcement officer whose primary job was to issue speeding tickets on state highways.

Alabama state law was ambiguous on issues relating to the enforcement powers of the Highway Patrol. The primary issue was whether Highway Patrol officers had the authority to engage in law enforcement activities outside the boundaries of state highways. Local police officers enforced the law within a city boundary, and county sheriffs within the boundaries of their county jurisdictions. State law officials such as game wardens, health inspectors, and marine police had jurisdiction only to the extent of the powers and duties prescribed by state law. It was generally presumed that there was no state law enforcement agency that had general law enforcement jurisdiction over the entire state. However, even before Daddy was elected, there were suggestions that the Highway Patrol should be given general jurisdiction throughout the state.

Lingo took advantage of the uncertainty of the situation and proclaimed that the Highway Patrol did in fact have general jurisdiction and that the newly named Alabama State Troopers had general law enforcement duties as directed by the governor. When neither he nor Daddy was challenged on the issue, Lingo became Alabama's most powerful law enforcement officer—answering to no one but Daddy.

THIS DEVELOPMENT SET the scene for the violent, heart-wrenching battles over civil rights during Daddy's first term. In the spring of 1963, after suffering a defeat in attempts to desegregate public facilities and schools in Albany, Georgia, Dr. Martin Luther King Jr. searched for the right place and moment to remind the world once again of the harsh reality of the American apartheid. Dr. King and the civil rights movement were at a crossroads. He had not won a major civil rights struggle in the seven years since the Montgomery bus boycott had ended. The time had come. His crusade would be called "Project C," for confrontation.

King chose Birmingham, the largest industrial city in the South, for his new campaign, a city where African Americans had been terrorized by the KKK for years. Blacks called Birmingham "Bombingham." They called one of their neighborhoods "Dynamite Hill." They were targeted by white terrorists, and the perpetrators always went unpunished. The white community blamed these incidents on black "agitators" seeking to "stir up" a black population who were supposedly just fine with their lot in life and were patiently waiting on the white man's largesse.

The day after the city election runoff, April 3, King called for lunch counter sit-ins in downtown Birmingham. Twenty protesters were arrested.

On April 12, Good Friday, the *Birmingham News* published a statement written by clergymen concerning the city's state of affairs as it related to the black issue. Although admitting that there was systematic segregation within the city, the ministers' letter condemned outsider influence and suggested that the matter should be the subject of civil discourse and legal action if necessary. They opposed civil disobedience of the kind that had been visited on their fair city.

That afternoon, Dr. King and Ralph Abernathy led a retinue of black ministers into the city's streets. Local and state law enforcement officers attacked the crowds of African Americans who stood on the shaded sidewalks to watch the peaceful march. King, Abernathy, and many others were arrested and jailed.

As King sat in solitary confinement, he wrote his famous "Letter from Birmingham Jail" in the margins of the *Birmingham News* in which the white Birmingham ministers had published their letter:

> I have traveled the length and breadth of Alabama, Mississippi and all the other southern states. On sweltering summer days and crisp autumn mornings I have looked at the South's beautiful churches with their lofty spires pointing heavenward. I have beheld the impressive outlines of her massive religious education buildings. Over and over I have found myself asking: "What kind of people worship here? Who is their God?... Where were they when Governor Wallace gave a clarion call for defiance and hatred? Where were their voices of support when bruised and weary Negro men and women decided to rise from the dark dungeons of complacency to the bright hills of creative protest?"

And then there was Al Lingo. According to one of Daddy's closest friends, Oscar Harper, Daddy issued a direct order to Lingo to stay away from Birmingham. But despite Daddy's directive, Lingo deployed state troopers and joined forces with the

Birmingham police commissioner, Bull Connor. However, Daddy did not fire Lingo for this transgression, perhaps because of his deep-seated angst over losing political allies.

Angry mobs of low-income men and women and the KKK were not the only supporters of segregation in Birmingham. On the crest of Birmingham's Red Mountain, in mansions with gorgeous views of downtown Birmingham, the old-line families and business magnates were more than happy for these ruffians to do what they would not stoop to do. George Wallace was not *their* kind of governor; there was not a whit of gentility or refinement in either his personality or pedigree. And yet many of them had secretly voted for him, and they were more than a little pleased with his constant railing against out-of-state black and white civil rights "agitators."

On April 26, U.S. Attorney General Robert F. Kennedy, accompanied by the head of the Justice Department's Civil Rights Division, Burke Marshall, arrived in Montgomery to meet with Daddy to discuss the integration of the University of Alabama. Before their arrival, Daddy ordered that the Confederate battle flag be raised on the dome of the state capitol. (It would remain there until 1991, and only on January 4, 1993, was it forever banned from flying above the capitol.)

On May 2 in Birmingham, more than one thousand children were arrested and hauled away to jail for demonstrating not far from the 16th Street Baptist Church. As additional children came to take their place the next day, Bull Connor ordered that fire hoses and police dogs be used to disperse the crowd. A photograph of an African American teenager standing in a seemingly penitent/passive pose as a snarling German shepherd ripped at his clothes was published in newspapers the following day. That photograph shifted the national perception of what was happening in the South and captured the essence of King's beliefs about the power of nonviolent confrontation. Who could not be outraged and moved?

On Monday, June 10, Daddy left the Governor's Mansion on his way to Tuscaloosa to prepare for what he believed would be seen as his finest hour: his literal stand in the schoolhouse door. Although his advisers disagreed as to the appropriateness of what he was planning, everyone knew his attempt to block two African American students, Vivian Malone and James Hood, from enrolling in the University of Alabama would fail. Daddy, though, saw it as an opportunity to fulfill his promise to Alabamians and show that his commitment to protect the culture of segregation was real.

Daddy was at ease and spoke glibly as a film crew followed him around the mansion prior to his departure. Footage shows the mansion foyer and sitting rooms. My father points out two portraits hanging on the wall, two Southern heroes of the Civil War, and extols their nobility and character. The camera traces his steps into the kitchen where the African American staff prepares our dinner. He descends to the mansion's rear parking area and waves to a line of African American men dressed in white uniforms, some leaning on what appear to be hoes and rakes. Daddy waves and they wave back. He notes to the camera that all of the African American men who are working in the mansion are convicts. Daddy smiles as he climbs into a car and drives away.

Following Daddy's departure from the Governor's Mansion, Mama took us to our house on Lake Martin. It was a simple cottage on stilts painted green overlooking the huge lake, about a forty-five-minute drive from Montgomery. This was Mama's retreat. She swam and fished, scaling and cleaning and cooking the fish herself. We had a powerboat. She taught me to water-ski, loved the sport herself and was good at it, weaving gracefully behind the boat in sweeping, measured curves. It was a place that offered her a reminder of how her life used to be living alongside the broken road. The cottage was her spiritual refuge, and my father appeared there only under duress.

The morning after we arrived at the lake, I watched Mama pace up and down, first on the pier, then on the screened-in front porch. It was as if a taut wire was dragging her about as she pulled one hand through her mane of thick brown hair while nursing a cigarette in the other. A small black-and-white TV was her only connection to the outside world. She was not able to watch it herself, too nervous that there would be violence and Daddy would be hurt. One of her security guards gave her updates as the scene unfolded in Tuscaloosa. I remember her palpable fear that day, a fear that became instilled in me. I, too, felt afraid that Daddy would be hurt. Later, the assassinations of John and Robert Kennedy and Martin Luther King Jr. would add to the feeling of unease and impending peril, as did the aura of hatred and bigotry that often surrounded my father's political rallies.

Mama's usual security detail of one had grown to a cadre of state troopers. Yet she stood alone, separate and apart from the universe of Daddy's politics. She was thirty-six. After that day, we would forever stand in the shadow of the schoolhouse door. And the grandchildren she would never know would one day ask *why?*

DADDY'S STAND IN the schoolhouse door at the University of Alabama had everything to do with the long sweep of Southern history and politics. For most white folks in Alabama, and for that matter throughout the South, Daddy was a twentieth-century Robert E. Lee. In the aftermath of the Confederate surrender at Appomattox, the white Southerners who remained standing amid the tattered flags of defeat felt ennobled. They passed down from generation to generation their hatred for those who had brought utter destruction to their doorsteps in the 1860s. The mere thought of the progeny of the slaves they once owned wanting to go to white schools and to sit down to eat with white people and, most appallingly, to *vote* was just more than most white folks could stand. Governor Wallace was going to put those modern-day carpetbaggers, socialists, and bigwigs who thought they were better than Southern white working folks in their place.

THE MONTHS LEADING up to June 11 had been violent across the South. Shouting mobs of white men, women, and children. Gunshots fired in the night. Campus riots erupted in the fall of 1962 at Ole Miss over the enrollment of James Meredith. Two people were killed and more than three hundred injured.

To my father's credit, all this weighed heavily on him, and he was determined that the violence and mayhem that had occurred at Ole Miss would not be repeated in his state and on his watch. Toward that end, he struck a Faustian bargain with the Klan and other white supremacist groups around Tuscaloosa County. They would stand down so that he could stand up for them and for the honor of all true Southerners. Southern pride dictated that even though he lost the battle, it didn't matter: it was the fact that he was willing to fight.

He said he had made his "stand" to forestall the violence that had happened in September at Ole Miss. Daddy went on state-wide TV and told people to keep away from Tuscaloosa. "I'm going to handle it," he said. He negotiated with the Klan and got them to step down. Was this a principled stand to try to avert violence, or playing for political advantage? Perhaps both? I'll never know for sure. Perhaps the fact that Daddy took the heat and diverted the anger of white Southerners was enough to justify what he did, but the world saw a Southern racist.

Historians agree that Daddy's "stand" was an orchestrated event agreed upon by him and the Kennedy administration. It would allow him to have his say. Everyone involved recognized that despite this "stand," Vivian Malone and James Hood would be able to peacefully register at the University of Alabama. In the broader sweep of history and the fight for racial equality, it was just one more act in the deadly theatrics that summer. There was no turning back for him; the arc of his moral universe was set. He was now a national figure, but he was on the wrong side of history.

Daddy knew that there was no winning of the war, but in his life and in his culture, there was no shame in losing as long as you stayed in the ring until you lay beaten and bloodied on the floor.

It was the fight for the Confederacy, and it was my father and uncles pounding one another in the living room in Clio while their drunken father egged them on and their mother, whose own mother had abandoned her and sent her to live in orphanage, looked on and said nothing.

On the night before the confrontation, Daddy stayed in a Tuscaloosa hotel. The next morning, he dressed in a gray suit and a brown-and-blue tie and got in his chauffeured old Ford to be driven over to Foster Auditorium, where 125 state police and revenue and game agents, 150 journalists, and a national television audience waited for a moment that many believed would end up with Daddy being arrested and possibly a full-scale riot. It was a sweltering hundred degrees. Daddy had a lectern placed in front of the door that Vivian Malone and James Hood would have to pass through to register for classes.

When the cars carrying the Washington officials and the students arrived, U.S. Deputy Attorney General Nicholas Katzenbach met my father and began reading a proclamation signed by President Kennedy calling on Daddy to end his defiance. Daddy interrupted him: "We don't need your speech," he said, and launched into his own speech, which had been written by Asa Carter:

> I stand before you here today in place of thousands of other Alabamians whose presence would have confronted you had I been derelict and neglected to fulfill the responsibilities of my office. It is the right of every citizen, however humble he may be, through his chosen officials of representative government to stand

courageously against whatever he believes to be the exercise of power beyond the Constitutional rights conferred upon our Federal Government.

"I don't know what the purpose of this show is . . . I ask you once again to responsibly step aside," Katzenbach said when Daddy was done. Daddy didn't budge. Katzenbach turned, walked down the steps, and got into the car where Malone and Hood sat waiting. The two students were driven to college dorms. Malone had lunch in the cafeteria, where she was warmly welcomed by many students.

After listening to Daddy's speech with mounting anger, Attorney General Robert Kennedy decided to nationalize the Alabama National Guard and send them on campus to see if that would end Daddy's posturing. In the afternoon, Daddy stepped outside again in front of the cameras. When National Guard General Henry V. Graham told him it was his duty to use the guard to force Daddy to back off, Daddy ranted about a "military dictatorship" in the United States. "We shall now return to Montgomery," he said in his exit line, "to continue this constitutional fight."

THE NEXT BATTLEGROUNDS lay ahead. Daddy deployed hundreds of state troopers to the far corners of the state with orders to close any public schools that tried to enroll children of color.

In Birmingham, three schools were closed; Lingo and six hundred state troopers stood watch. Game wardens, food inspectors, county and local law enforcement personnel, prison guards, and other state workers were pressed into service and donned the uniform of Alabama state troopers. The financial burden on the state was enormous but was never mentioned or discussed. Daddy was in complete control and no state department heads or agencies dared to stand in his way.

As Birmingham schools were closed one by one, white students, their parents, and local townspeople rode the streets and stood on benches in front of schools, waving Confederate flags and hurling racial epithets at passersby. Jack Cash, a member of the KKK, was arrested near Ramsey High School when local police found guns, flares, and a meat hook in his car.

Amid the chaos, Daddy spoke at a Labor Day picnic in Birmingham. "We are not fighting against the Negro people, we are fighting for local government and states' rights." At the same time, in some areas of Alabama there was an increasing number of school boards and elected officials that were weary and fearful and had come to the realization that perhaps it would be better to concede the issue and admit African American students to their local schools rather than bend to the will of their governor's crusade.

Daddy could feel this softening. Under the guise of maintaining peace and tranquility, he would strike first, before local elected officials and law enforcement could concede. He promoted the notion that the use of intimidation and violence was simply to maintain order and protect the safety of both black and white law-abiding citizens. On September 2, he sent state troopers to maintain order in Tuskegee and more particularly at Tuskegee High School. The county board of education was firm in its statement that there had been no threat of violence and stated that the schools would be integrated as scheduled. In spite of the decision of the board to move forward with integration, Daddy refused to accept their decision. He would have no part of it.

BUT THE WORST was yet to come. On Sunday, September 15, the 16th Street Baptist Church at the corner of Sixth Avenue and Sixteenth Street in downtown Birmingham sat quiet as its African American congregation gathered. There was no reason to fear during precious moments of being in God's house where no harm would surely come.

The sun was peeking from behind the clouds at ten twenty-two that morning. Sunday school had ended. Members of the congregation were enjoying moments of conversation and fellowship. Four young girls were still on the ground floor beneath the sanctuary where their Sunday school classes met. There was no escape, no time to say goodbye when fifteen sticks of dynamite exploded.

Carol Denise McNair, eleven years old, and Carole Robertson, Cynthia Wesley, and Addie Mae Collins, all fourteen years old, were killed. Addie Mae's younger sister, twelve-year-old Sarah, suffered serious injuries and was blinded in one of her eyes. Deep in my heart I believed they were like me, innocent children with probably little or no concept of the larger forces of history and hatred that would end their lives. They didn't choose the cruel honor of becoming martyrs for a righteous cause.

After the bombing, outrage erupted in the city. Before the day was over, a policeman had shot and killed sixteen-year-old

Johnny Robinson after he was caught throwing rocks at cars and ran when the police ordered him to stop. Thirteen-year-old Virgil Ware was shot and killed by two Eagle Scouts while he was riding his bike.

Virgil Ware and I were the same age. How would my mama have felt if it had been me? And what would my father have done to the man that let it happen? Those were the questions that I should have asked.

ON FRIDAY, NOVEMBER 22, I wore a short-sleeved jumper; the forecast promised a sunny day with record-breaking temperatures in the low eighties. As usual, an Alabama state trooper, assigned to the mansion detail, drove me to school. Daddy left before me, heading first to his office at the capitol before flying to Haleyville in north Alabama to speak at the dedication of a new high school.

After almost a year of demonstrations and violence, I hoped that with the coming of winter there would be better days ahead. Our first Thanksgiving in the Governor's Mansion was less than a week away. Mamaw and Mr. Henry were coming on Sunday to spend the week and share our good fortune.

It was just past two. I was sitting in my math class. The principal's voice came on over the school intercom. "Students, can I have your attention? Please let me have your attention." Then there was nothing. It sounded like someone was gasping for air. "We have just been informed that President Kennedy was shot and killed at one o'clock this afternoon in Dallas, Texas."

Our teacher sat stunned in her desk chair. She did not notice the state trooper who had entered the room. My classmates turned toward me. Curiosity? Perhaps pity? Or were their eyes accusing? I gathered my things, stared straight ahead, and followed the trooper to the car.

As we approached the mansion gates, I turned my face away when I saw a group of reporters, some with cameras, in front of the mansion. The trooper pulled around in back, and I walked up the steps and into the kitchen, where there were usually bustling cooks. Now, no one. The maids who seemed to always be on the move had disappeared as well. The mansion lay quiet and low.

I walked upstairs. A television offered the only light in the darkened family room. Mama was sitting in a straight-backed chair, staring at the television screen. Standing around her were the African American cooks, maids, and groundskeepers who lived and worked at the mansion. Everyone was crying.

11

Picture Perfect

*The excursion is the same when you go looking for your
sorrow as when you go looking for your joy.*

—*Eudora Welty*

After that dark moment, in the early days of 1964, living behind the gates of the Governor's Mansion, I felt optimistic and hopeful. Our family was often all together, and I had the kind of life that I had always imagined my friends had. When Daddy was home, I felt no obligation to challenge him on issues relating to his politics of race and segregation, although by this point I knew that his politics would never be my politics and that they ran counter to what I knew in every fiber of my being was just and kind.

I know that I was only fourteen, but now, looking back, I sometimes wonder if I should have stood against my father. Did my birthright obligate me to do more? Was I lost in the trappings of the advantages I now see? It seemed to me that we had burst into glorious bloom. Should I have felt uneasy standing amid so much grief with a smile on my face?

ONE OF THE things I distinctly recall about this period is that Mama became confident in herself. It was a time for her to reap the benefits from her many years investing in and believing in Daddy. He had promised that one day he would be governor of Alabama and he had delivered.

Mama began to gather a small group of friends around her. They were a mix of women from Clayton who, along with their husbands, had followed us to Montgomery, others she met during the campaign, and the wives of our security detail. Some of the husbands would reap the rewards of being within the Wallace circle, but Mama's friends expected nothing of her in return other than enjoying being in her company, and, of course, gossiping about the endless intrigues of the Wallace family.

Early in her career as a candidate's wife, Mama grew accustomed to women in Sunday dresses with matching hats making small talk. Crystal punch bowls sat on dining room tables. There were green, yellow, and pink party mints and finger sandwiches. To most of the exclusively female guests at this endless string of events, it would have been grossly impolite to launch into the matter of politics—that was a man's job. And for other women, there was always the potential for embarrassment should they become flushed and tongue-tied while talking to Mama about her handsome, powerful, charismatic husband.

After moving into the Governor's Mansion, Mama expected me to attend the teas and receptions when I was available and at home. "Peggy Sue, this is good practice for you. Stand over here by me and introduce yourself to the guests as they shake your hand."

I was amazed at Mama's ability to always make people comfortable. She had a knack for pulling people in with a smile or finding common ground. I often heard her say "I know just what you mean" or "I would have done the same thing."

Her down-home style of clothing and her affinity for store-bought jewelry were looked down on by more fashion-conscious women. But she was mostly embraced as someone who was just "like one of us." Even Daddy sometimes commented on how popular Mama had become.

THERE WAS ONE woman who was particularly close to Mama. During the 1962 campaign, Mama met Sybil Simon at a house party in Montgomery. Her husband was in the liquor business and managed a local country club. Sybil was worldly in a sophisticated Southern way. She had impeccable manners and was a wonderful storyteller, a Steel Magnolia kind of woman. Like Mama, she wore gloves to church and would then sit out in the backyard drinking whiskey in pedal pushers while playing poker. She and Mama would float out on the lake on inner tubes with cold beers in their hands. They were caustic, hilarious, and tough. Sybil's skin was ruddy and tanned. She was always on the move and she spoke with a gravelly Southern accent. She was an observer of other people—from a distance. Some found her to be too direct, getting to the point without meaningless chatter. She preferred menthol cigarettes and midafternoon and early evening cocktails over bridge and tea cakes and champagne. She was less enthralled with Daddy than most.

Sybil and Mama were both rugged and no-nonsense beneath their sheeps' coats of Southern gentility. While they often stood in the shadow of their husbands, they knew who was really in charge. I used to hear Sybil say, "Just let him think he's in charge so he will stay out of our way." After Mama died, Sybil Simon was always there to remind me of who Mama was.

NOT LONG AFTER their first meeting, Sybil came to work at the mansion as Mama's secretary. Mama would often sit on a small French sofa besides Sybil's desk to while away what little free time she may have had.

On one side of the fireplace there was a wall cabinet that was not readily visible to a casual observer. It became the perfect place for Sybil and Mama to store a stash of bourbon and scotch. Although Daddy had specifically promised to the voters that there would be no liquor in the mansion as long as he was governor, Mama and Sybil regularly had cocktails in either the office or just outside on the wide veranda overlooking the mansion grounds. Sybil would talk with Mama about anything but Daddy; she was wise to hold her tongue. However, whether spoken or not, she surmised early on that her employer's husband had a mean streak a mile long.

Sybil's husband, James, was still in the bar business and managing a local country club when Sybil came to work at the mansion. The country club pool became a regular hangout for my girlfriends and me in the summers of 1963 and 1964. In 1965,

James suffered a stroke that left him partially paralyzed and out of a job. Sybil approached Daddy and asked him if he would consider appointing James to the Alabama Alcoholic Beverage Control Board, which would have provided him with a paycheck and insurance for his family. It would have been different if James was not qualified, couldn't be trusted, or was a bumbling fool. But Daddy's denial came with a "Can't do it, his name sounds too Jewish." It was not political, not anti-Semitic in the broader sense. He said it because he could; it was cruel and hateful and he knew that it was. When Daddy was in private, there was always a fine line between saying what he meant and just being mean-spirited and in a foul mood—and it was often difficult to discern which was which.

WITH SYBIL'S HELP, Mama delivered on her promise to open the Governor's Mansion to the public. Volunteers usually ushered tours. Mama made it a point, however, to be available when students were scheduled to visit. Mama had a genuine affection for young people and enjoyed having the opportunity to show them through her new home. To the students' delight, it was not uncommon for my sister Lee to bound through them or play on the foyer staircase while Mama was conducting a tour.

Mama's simple affect and her deep-South drawl made her at times the butt of jokes by those who could not see beyond her upbringing as a farmer's daughter. Her reluctance to walk among the educated class, due to her own lack of a formal education beyond high school, encouraged her to perfect her warmth and country grace. The overwhelming majority of working-class men and women in Alabama saw in Mama a reflection of their own selves. She came to understand that what one sees in oneself is not always as important as what others see in you.

As Mama rose to new heights of popularity, her detractors fell silent. They came to see that the very traits of hers about which they had complained, her style and character, propelled her to new heights of power and prestige. My mama's humble beginnings became a living testament to working-class mothers and fathers that the circumstances of their daughters' birth had little to do with how far in life they could climb.

It became generally understood among Montgomery's women of society that it was best to confine their discussions about the persona of Lurleen Wallace to their country club powder rooms. For although it was an absolute given that none of their husbands would ever be the object of Mama's affection, the globe-trotting wives were totally flummoxed when it dawned on them that the husbands would prefer to hunt and fish with Lurleen Wallace than dine on fine china and make small talk with their more elegant wives.

My mama was an extraordinary woman—completely authentic and lacking in pretense. She was clear-eyed and rang true. And to this day I miss her.

WOULDN'T YOU KNOW it. Following on the heels of his notoriety after his stand in the schoolhouse door, Daddy turned his attention to the national stage. In February 1964, he concluded a third national speaking tour, which had captured more free media than any other politician in the country. On March 17, Daddy qualified to run in the Democratic presidential primary in Wisconsin. With less than a month to campaign, the political prognosticators gave him little chance of success. On April 7, the date of the primary, Daddy received a quarter million votes. It was the beginning of his presidential aspirations, and Alabamians were proud. On April 14 we were at the Montgomery airport, where an estimated three thousand Alabamians gathered to welcome him home.

Folks were proud that their homegrown governor had become a national political force, standing up to liberals, hippies, and overindulged college kids at every Ivy League college in America (except Yale, where those Communist professors, no doubt, were just too scared to let him even set foot on their campus). But his detractors and the press saw in him a seeming lack of interest in doing the job he was elected to do, and that gave them something to complain about. For Mama and the rest of us it was nothing new: his extended absences from home were a given in our lives.

Even the Governor's Mansion couldn't lure him home. Mama was in charge. While I was always happy to hear Daddy's footsteps on the back stairs of the mansion at the end of the day, it was never a surprise when there was nothing but silence. We had to accept him for who he was.

Even with his family surrounding him—when you would have thought he would feel safest and calmest and most content and loved—he became quickly uneasy and off balance. In his mind he was still alone. He drew his brand of self-assurance from strangers and hangers-on rather than from us. But the mansion did give him an incentive to politick at home. There was room to move about, gated grounds to walk through, and a veranda to sit on while stabbing at the dark with the end of a glowing cigar to make a point. The first floor offered quiet and elegant surroundings that were of no particular interest to Daddy but could become a useful tool of persuasion for others.

Despite his ruffian style, Daddy looked as if he had always been the master of the stately mansion when he descended the grand staircase to greet awestruck guests standing below. There were always people around, someone to talk to or stand outside with while smoking a Garcia y Vega cigar.

The mansion's living quarters on the second floor had a lived-in look with rather plain furniture, family pictures on the walls, and a variety of knickknacks that Mama had retrieved from Clayton and placed on end tables and bookcase shelves. An open mezzanine on the second floor divided the living quarters in half and served as our den. It became a perfect vantage point for eavesdropping on private conversations below. On both sides of the balcony, bedroom doors opened onto central halls that were visible from downstairs. There was often no privacy. I was often reminded that I should be appropriately dressed and groomed when I stepped through my bedroom door while tours were being conducted. Mama said it was but a small price to pay for the opportunity to live in such a grand place.

WITHOUT THE BURDEN of impending financial ruin facing Mama, her relationship with Daddy improved. However, they still battled, Mama snapping at Daddy's heels as he sought either truce or shelter. Following their reconciliation in 1960, Mama and Daddy came to an understanding that if Daddy won the governor's race in 1962, the office would belong to both of them. They agreed to be partners in the family-owned business of selling the Wallace brand, but each reserved the right to have days off. Mama pursued her interest in hunting, fishing, and being with friends, while Daddy ran the state without Mama looking over his shoulder.

All of us would have been hard-pressed to make a list of Daddy's friends: they were few and mostly invisible. His political intimates and allies were advisers but hardly friends. Perhaps the closest he came to friendship as most would define the term were his state trooper security guards who stood by him for the many years he was governor and, later in life, the African American men who cared for him as he lay mostly inert and in constant pain.

In Daddy's dictionary there was no such word as *relaxation*. He was not one to just sit idle. When he felt obligated to join us in front of the television or was called to listen to a favorite song playing on the record player, his restlessness and fidgeting would usually result in Mama's telling him to just get up and go on about his business. His ability to sit still generally lasted about as long as it took for him to get all the sugar out of a piece of Juicy Fruit chewing gum before he spat it out.

When Daddy was home, he prowled. He seemed to always be searching for something in his pockets or rummaging through the stack of newspapers spread out around his chair. He was notorious for calling people at all times of the day or night and often had to convince the person who picked up the phone that it was indeed Governor Wallace on the line. A long cord installed on a phone next to the family dining room allowed him to talk, pace, and eat at the same time. He usually kept his shirt and tie on until bedtime.

And yet Daddy would occasionally leave off politicking and become a kind and funny husband and father. These were moments when I glimpsed the young man with big dreams and unabashed enthusiasm for life that Mama had met, fallen in love with, and married.

There were nights at the mansion when Mama and Daddy would dance to Loretta Lynn's "Before I'm Over You" or Hank Williams's "Long Gone Lonesome Blues" playing on the stereo. Daddy would sometimes stiffen and draw Mama close if he felt they were out of step. There were moments when Mama twirled away with her left hand extended before curling back into Daddy's arms, laying her cheek to his. Dancing inspired moments of intimacy without the risk of emotional entanglement. And for most of my life, that is what I thought love was all about.

I GREW SLOWLY used to this new life with its predictable rhythms. I became part of a clique without even knowing what a clique was. I was suddenly popular, always in a hurry and running late. I no longer had to envy girls my age when I saw them shopping with their mothers or overheard them talking about their weekend plans for sleepovers, because my life was becoming like theirs. For the first time I believed I had the right to be happy.

In the spring of 1965 I graduated from Bellingrath Junior High School. At the age of fifteen, I was nothing like the painfully shy twelve-year-old girl who walked to school with her brother each morning. The glass slipper of good fortune fit perfectly on my foot. Following the ceremony's closing prayer, Daddy and Mama moved slowly through the crowd as people came up to greet them. On the school's front lawn, I was surrounded by friends until a state trooper retrieved me. "Your Mama and Daddy want to get a picture of you before y'all leave," he said, pointing his finger toward a gathering crowd. "They're somewhere in there!"

Daddy saw me first and waved his hand in the air. "Sugah, come on over here and stand by us while we get a picture. These folks won't mind a bit." When I was within a few steps of where he and Mama were standing, he said to no one in particular, but to everyone within earshot, "You are a pretty little thing. Your Mama and I sure are proud." I glowed inside.

"God just bless all you Wallaces," someone called. "We just love everything about you."

And then an elderly man stepped forward and said the kind of thing that killed that glow and had begun more and more to disturb me. "I got a granddaughter that graduated today," he said as he jostled himself to the front of the crowd.

"Well, that's mighty fine," Daddy replied.

"Yep, her mama and grandmamma think so." The man leaned in closer. "Yeah, and I'm just glad you kept the blacks out of here." *They belong here too*, I said to myself. *They are my brothers and sisters and I want them at my side.*

The photographer asked the crowd to move back a few steps so he could set the shot. "Peggy, let's put you on the end with the

Me and Daddy, Mama, and Janie Lee at my graduation from
Bellingrath Junior High School, May 1965.

governor beside you. Mrs. Wallace, you stand next to the governor and we will let the little one stand in front."

Daddy put his arm around me and pulled me close to him. Just before the camera flashed, a woman in the crowd said, "Now, that is picture-perfect!"

A Storm's a-Comin'

*My dear, I think of you always and at night I build myself
a warm nest of things I remember and float in your
sweetness till morning.*

—*Zelda Fitzgerald*

The Fort Morgan Road in Gulf Shores, Alabama, is twenty-three miles long and ends at the mouth of Mobile Bay. When I was a child, the road to Fort Morgan was barely touched by civilization. Occasional wood-framed houses painted in summer pastels rose on creosote poles above sugar-white sand, strung out along otherwise desolate beaches. Empty trailers hitched to the backs of pickup trucks sat along the road's shoulder near primitive boat launches on the bay. Seabirds sat atop the stumps of washed-away piers.

In the spring of 1963, Lamar Little, a Louisiana real estate developer, and his partners constructed a 7,500-square-foot, two-story cinder block mansion along the shoreline of the Gulf and deeded it to Daddy. In turn, Daddy deeded it to the state with the stipulation that it would be for the exclusive use of Alabama governors. It became a summer retreat for our family. A ten-foot concrete wall on the west side of the house provided privacy and security while the east side faced nothing but miles of sand dunes. The property's desolation and a beachfront devoid of people was part of its allure for Mama. Along with the lake house, it became a refuge.

I GRUMBLED IN the early summer of 1965 when Mama told me we were going to the Beach Mansion for an extended stay. My declarations to Mama that she was ruining my life and that I should be allowed to stay in Montgomery at the Governor's Mansion were met with stone-faced rejection. "You are completely boy crazy," she said. "And I don't trust your daddy to keep an eye on you." As a last-ditch effort, I reminded her that she and Daddy were married when she was sixteen. Bending her head a bit so that she could look at me over the top of her reading glasses, she replied, "I rest my case."

Mamaw and Mr. Henry went with us along with Mama's new secretary, Catherine Steineker, who carried with her the 1962 edition of *Amy Vanderbilt's Complete Book of Etiquette* everywhere she went. There would never be a table setting mishap, or a thank-you note not handwritten, as long as Catherine was around.

At the beach, Mama woke early and walked the shoreline. The love of solitary sunrises had been a part of Mama's life since she was a child. Her feet were always the first ones to hit the floor in the morning. As for Daddy, he preferred to get up a bit later. I have mentioned that even on Christmas mornings, Mama always sat alone to cheer our good fortune as we plundered through gifts under the tree. Cheerfulness among young children with their Christmas oohs, aahs, and "Look what Santa brought me" in the early morning hours was more than Daddy could bear. He finally appeared about noon. "That's mighty fine, mighty fine, sugah," he wanly said as I showed off my spoils. "Wonder how much that set Santa back?"

After her morning walks, Mama returned to the grounds of the Beach Mansion and with a cup of coffee in her hand watched sand crabs skitter into freshly excavated holes just to the north of small piles of broken shells that marked the high tide line. Driftwood lay in the dunes. Mama pocketed unbroken sand dollars. After breakfast every morning, Mama and Mr. Henry set up umbrellas and beach chairs and planted two eight-foot casting rods in sand spikes just out of the waves' reach. Mama set her tackle box on top of a metal ice chest filled with frozen shrimp and cut bait. She tied weights to fishing lines as Mr. Henry studied the current.

"Mutt, come up here and help me find the flow. The tide is right but the water is slow. We need to find the trough that's taking those fish in and out of town."

Mama took off her sunglasses and covered her eyes with her hand. "Just look straight out a ways. See it?"

"Not yet."

Mama took Mr. Henry's chin in her hand and slowly moved it to the left. "Look straight ahead. Where that bird just dove."

"See it now! Ready to catch some fish?"

Mama smiled and patted Mr. Henry on the cheek. "Those fish don't stand a chance when Mutt and Daddy are in town."

By the time Mamaw pulled herself together and settled on the beach, Mama and Mr. Henry had caught enough fish for supper.

"I quit cleaning fish long ago," Mamaw grumbled. "I'm going to sit right here, have a cigarette and a Seven-Up and watch out for Peggy Sue in that water."

Building driftwood fires in the sand was one of the things I enjoyed most about being with Mama at the Beach Mansion; even I couldn't put a sourpuss on such romantic fun. It was also a treat to see Mama so carefree.

ONE NIGHT TOWARD the end of our stay, Mama sat in front of the driftwood blaze, her knees pulled up tight against her, gazing into the heart of the flames. She was quiet and pensive, a contrast to her gently ebullient mood of recent weeks. My grandparents came out of the house and down to the beach to join us. They settled into chairs set low in the sand. The fire blew this way and that. "The wind's picking up," Mamaw said after a while. Mr. Henry threw some more wood on the fire. My mama was so still, so removed. It made me uneasy. Perhaps she was thinking about all that Daddy had done. A recent poll showed the mood of the country turning toward civil rights and against Daddy. She knew the trip to the beach was coming to an end and that she would have to return and once again step into the role of Alabama's First Lady.

Thunder rolled over the black water. The wind rose. Gusts carried spray from the surf roaring up the beach. The top of a styrofoam ice chest missed Mamaw's head only by inches as it cartwheeled into the dark.

"Come on y'all, grab all your stuff, we got to get up and get in," Mamaw said.

Still, Mama didn't move. She sat as if in a trance. Lightning stabbed the restless Gulf and thunder pounded us. Mama didn't flinch.

"Lurleen, you need to get up!" Mamaw yelled. She tugged on Mama's arm. "A storm's a-comin', and we need to get on home."

13

Success Is to Succeed

*I used to get things done by saying please. Now I dynamite
'em out of my path.*

—*Huey Long*

Daddy's lifelong ambition of being governor was not just for
one four-year term. The problem was that the Alabama
Constitution of 1819 prohibited the governor from succeeding
himself.

In Daddy's mind, he needed a second term for the purpose of
fueling the engine of his presidential aspirations. Without a
second term, he wouldn't have a strong platform to run on. In
retrospect, I can say without a doubt that our family's situation
and finances—where we would live and what we would live off of
if he was out of office—never entered his mind.

Still riding high among whites for his "stand," in June 1963,
Daddy suggested to his legislative allies that it was time to pass a
succession amendment and let the voters decide if they wanted

to keep him around for four more years. The proposal did not pass. The second time around, in August 1964, the same thing happened. While members of the house of representatives were easy to manage, there was a group of recalcitrant state senators who seemed impervious to his shouted demands, determined to stop the Wallace Roadshow before it became the Wallace Dynasty. By September 1965, time was running out. The hoped-for "third time's a charm" special session was called to order on October 4, less than seven months before the gubernatorial primary. By that time there were no bonds of civility left in the Alabama state capitol between the warring factions of Daddy's men and his opponents.

Daddy stood in the well of the Alabama house of representatives. Packed crowds in the gallery above waved signs and acted intemperately with hoots, hollers, and heel-stomping. "Let the people decide," Daddy said.

> Why do liberal newspaper editors so viciously attack the idea that the governor might succeed himself? The answer is easy. The liberals want the state destroyed, all power and all benefits to come from a centralized government. They want us to quit doing and start begging. I believe in the cause of freedom. The people of Alabama sent me north and east and west to tell the story of Americanism in the South. It would have been easy to remain in Montgomery in comfort and in peace, but because I believe in the cause of freedom I have gone among wild-eyed fanatics. I have walked through stomping crowds of leftists and I have been cursed by

them and I have been beat upon and their spittle has
run down my face.

Wallace supporters fled from the capitol into the night, ready
to fight for four more years. Daddy's judge and jury were the
people of Alabama, and they had his back. They thought it
perfectly reasonable for Daddy to defund road projects, cancel
contracts, move the location of a proposed junior college to the
other end of the state, and pull liquor advertising from newspapers if that is what it took to whip the troublemakers that
disagreed with him back into shape. After all, families stick
together, and Governor Wallace was family.

Once again, the succession bill bullied its way through the
House but was held up in the Alabama senate with a filibuster. On
October 22, 1965, the final vote to break the filibuster was
defeated by three votes. Daddy was both stunned and infuriated.
It never occurred to him that his behavior toward the holdouts
in the Senate had been counterproductive. He had launched
public tirades against them in their home districts. He had hurled
invective. He had threatened to make their constituents pay. This,
of course, had emboldened the rebellious senators to dig in their
heels.

In the end, from Daddy's perspective, it was not all about
whether he actually meant to do the things he threatened to do;
he just wanted to have his way, and unless the referee catches you
breaking the quarterback's finger in the pileup, it's just another
way to win. The 1965 defeat of the succession bill was personal.
Daddy viewed it as an attack on his character and fitness.
Rejection was not something he handled well.

None of the state senators who filibustered the succession bill to the end would be returned to service following the 1966 election; they either didn't run or were overwhelmingly defeated. However, in return for their sacrifice, Alabama would elect its first female governor, and the Wallace Dynasty was assured.

14

Dynasty

I've learned that people will forget what you said, people will forget what you did, but people will never forget how you made them feel.

—*Maya Angelou*

In the fall of 1965, while Daddy was at war with the Alabama legislature on the matter of gubernatorial succession, I was a freshman at Sidney Lanier High School, where a war of another kind was being fought. It was the year Delores Boyd and other African American students integrated my freshman class. Although there were no known or perceived threats to me, I was accompanied to school each day by a detail of state troopers.

While my bodyguards protected me, black students were accosted, isolated, and threatened with violence almost daily. Although my instincts invited me to welcome them, befriend them, and stand by them, I did nothing. All eyes seemed to be on me, watching to see what I would do as I witnessed bigotry and intimidation.

Although Daddy was in the midst of a fight for his political future that fall, he sometimes returned to the mansion for dinner. "How was school today, sugah?" he would ask. I could have reported on the treatment of my African American schoolmates. I said nothing. Each time he asked, I was silent. I lost the opportunity to become my better self and stand up for Delores, who would one day become my friend.

Instead, I became a joiner and a cheerleader, participating in the sort of activities that boastful parents roll out at neighborhood cookouts and pre–Sunday school chatter. Mama came to cheer me on during football nights, sometimes lingering to talk to my friends and their parents. She had such an easy, winning way about her, putting everyone at ease with her total lack of affectation and her warmth.

She stayed up until I came home on weekend nights after being out with friends. She told me how silly it was to cry every time I listened to Paul McCartney songs. My first official date arrived at the front door of the mansion. For a casual observer it would seem to be nothing more than normal family life, but for me it was much more. It was the beginning of the end of another cloverleaf necklace. These necklaces are something Southern girls weave from the clover growing in our yards. They signify good luck.

As Mamaw would say, "You dry them little necklaces in some tissue paper then put 'em up somewhere where you can remember, so maybe you can take 'em out and frame 'em one day when you get set up in a house of your own."

The enchanted life I was leading was about to end.

THE NIGHT OF the final vote on the succession bill, it was Albert Brewer, the Alabama house speaker and a friend, who called the mansion and asked for Mama. After exchanging brief greetings, Brewer told her that the succession bill failed for the third time. "Lurleen, there's a lot of talk up here about you running next time," he said.

Mama chuckled. Brewer could hear the click of her cigarette lighter. This was the first she had heard of this rather audacious idea. She gathered herself for a few moments and replied, "If anyone is going to run for governor, it's going to be you. Martha and I will hit the road and hold teas from one end of the state to the other."

"Well," said Brewer, "all I can say is you'd better get your running shoes on."

I remember Mama telling us the succession bill had failed. "Hold on, your daddy's coming home with thunder. Nothing you can do to fix it. Find a place to lay low."

SEVEN WEEKS FOLLOWING the defeat of the succession bill and two days before Thanksgiving, Mama received the results of a uterine biopsy from her doctor, Joe Perry. She had cancer. Her diagnosis led to radiation treatments in early December. Mamaw and Mr. Henry came for Christmas early, and Aunt Bill and her husband drove straight through from Sea Island, Georgia, on Christmas Eve. Mama was not going to allow her diagnosis to ruin her favorite time of the year.

Mama checked into the hospital on January 9, 1966. The next morning, a team of surgeons removed a malignant uterine tumor while performing a complete hysterectomy. While offering an optimistic prognosis following her surgery, Dr. Perry suggested that all the talk he was hearing about her running for governor should be put aside so that she could spend more time with family.

Perhaps Mama should have heeded Dr. Perry's advice. Enjoy one last year in Montgomery, spruce up the house in Clayton, go down home while Daddy ran for president, and settle in to die. On the other hand, if she were governor, she could exercise her own power, be one who could build, heal the sick, and encourage others. If she chose to leave the capitol and become a housewife again, none of that would happen. She must have wondered deep down if she would survive. She was thirty-nine years old.

By late January the word was out that she was in. Whether it was cigar smoke or high-heeled shoes, it didn't matter so long as it was a Wallace.

In late February, Mama called me to come upstairs. She patted the sofa cushion beside her. "You and I need to talk about something," she said. "Now hear me out before you say anything. I am thinking about running for governor. This is something I want to do."

My response was a clear, unequivocal *no*. I was afraid. There had been no conversations about Mama's surgery or what was facing her, much less the rest of us. The politics I had witnessed involved not the glory of winning and all that it could bring, but long nights on dark roads, loneliness, and neglect. There were always to-do lists of the important things that had to be done before anything could be done for me. For my entire life, Mama had been in the same boat with me. She was on my team of heartache. Mama understood that it was *politics* when they had to send someone back to pick me up because they had forgotten that I was even there. Now she wanted me to think it was okay for her to become the purveyor of sorrow in my life, rather than be the only one that thought of me first. Mama's promise that things would not change just because she would be governor fell on deaf ears. I felt betrayed when she said, "Just think, the campaign will be so much fun for you and me."

ON FEBRUARY 24, Mama announced her candidacy before an overflow crowd in the house chamber in the capitol. Wallace supporters came from all of Alabama's sixty-seven counties. Mama made some brief remarks; then Daddy took the stage. He rained down fire and brimstone, railing against the federal government, the federal courts, and any other "federal" he could think of. He knew how to raise the hackles of working-class and low-income white voters who were listening in by invoking "states' rights."

Even before the cheering stopped, most political prognosticators were ready to announce that Lurleen Wallace was not just the most popular candidate in the race—she might as well be the only candidate. "Anybody who runs against Lurleen Wallace is going

Mama at a campaign rally for governor, 1966.

to be wasting their time and somebody else's money," an old-line politician said. "George might have lost this race, but those SOBs who filibustered his succession bill are going to elect his wife."

"She is in it to win it," her supporters said. "When she gets elected, we will have two governors for the price of one. He is going to be her number one adviser. So it really don't make a hill of beans who is carrying the keys to the governor's office in her purse."

MAMA CAMPAIGNED FROM town to town through the spring of 1966. The crowds were loud and boisterous. Mrs. George C. Wallace became Mrs. Lurleen Burns Wallace and finally just Miss Lurleen. For every skeptical eye that looked crossways at her, there were thousands of weatherworn hands that reached out to shake the hand of their Lurleen. She was one of them.

Many observers saw Mama as a mere extension of Daddy's ambitions. Daddy could move a crowd into a state of hysteria. Mama portrayed herself as just like the people who came and stood in courthouse squares to hear her speak. Her common touch was a powerful political tool. She lingered in crowds to listen for as long as it took. She acted as if it was a privilege for her to shake someone's hand and to listen to them. She always had time for people. There was only one Lurleen.

Mama's presence rather than just her words gave her power. Daddy noticed. There was no doubt that he was proud of her emerging confidence.

I'm not sure exactly what the political agenda was that Daddy hoped Mama could accomplish. I think in large part he had her run because he was still aggrieved about losing on the issue of succession. He thought about those legislators who had voted against him—*I'll show you: Lurleen will run. Nobody is going to throw the Wallaces out in the road.*

And make no mistake—he did show them. But I don't think Daddy had counted on Mama being quite *so* capable and popular. His oversized ego bristled when he saw Mama swamped by admirers while he waited by the car. At times, it was just about more than Daddy could bear.

"Gerald, I want my own car and driver," Mama said in late March.

"Is George getting under your skin?"

"No, I'm getting under his. I think the man is jealous."

Gerald laughed. "He doesn't like to get upstaged."

"Well, he better get used to it!"

———

IN THE MAY Democratic primary, Mama bested ten other opponents without a runoff by receiving over 54 percent of all votes cast. In the general election, she carried sixty-five of Alabama's sixty-seven counties with 63 percent of the total vote. Her victory was stunning, and was a record Daddy hadn't equaled. While most of the votes were the result of white voters' affinity for Daddy's politics, there was no doubt that it was Lurleen Wallace herself who brought thousands of voters to the polls.

It was a sunny 46 degrees on January 19, 1967. Mama, wearing a tailor-made knee-length skirt and suit coat of black velvet with a white silk ascot and a pillbox hat, stood before an estimated crowd of a quarter million well-wishers who lined the streets of downtown Montgomery to view the largest inaugural parade in state history and witness the swearing in of Alabama's first female governor and its most beloved citizen. As Mama raised her right hand to take the oath of office, I gazed down from the capitol steps at the thousands of faces and heard their roars of approval. It was the day the Wallaces became the most powerful political family in the history of Alabama.

That night, Mama's friends and our family gathered at the mansion to celebrate our good fortune. After making sure that Daddy was in earshot, Mamaw leaned forward on the sofa she was sharing with Mr. Henry and Mama. "Well, George," she said. "This is for sure one time you can thank Lurleen for keeping a roof over your head and food on the table. Can't be any arguing about that anymore, now can there."

FOR THE FIRST five months of her term, Mama was engaged with the duties and obligations of her governorship. She passed a bond issue to improve mental health services and create the Alabama state parks system. But it was her character and purpose, her caring for the down and forgotten and the thousands of middle-class families, both whites and African Americans, who saw their own hopes and dreams in her life's story, that laid claim to the legacy she would leave behind.

"When your mother was governor, every Sunday after church my parents would ride my sister and me by the Governor's

The broken road touches history, Tuscaloosa, Alabama, 1967.

Mansion. Daddy would pull over for a minute or two," a friend of Mark's told me many years later. "My mother wanted my sister to know that Miss Lurleen lived there and that one day she could be a governor too."

Then, in June 1967, Mama's cancer returned. Hopeful and optimistic outlooks from her physicians and her friends encouraged her to fight on for her benefit and for ours. But in the early morning hours of May 7, 1968, just two weeks before I graduated from high school, Mama died at the age of forty-one. She had served as governor for only fifteen months.

Later that same day, her body was returned to the mansion. Her open casket was placed in the sitting room between the pair of floor-to-ceiling pier mirrors that faced each other. They were the same mirrors I stood between after Daddy's inaugural ball in 1963, only five years before, when I said to myself that a carefree, magical life was mine.

I stepped through my second-floor bedroom door and walked to the balcony rail. I saw Mama's reflection falling back on itself again and again.

"There was never any magic in this place at all," I thought to myself. I felt heartbroken and very much alone.

THE FOLLOWING DAY, Mama's body lay in state in the Alabama capitol rotunda. More than thirty thousand people stood in line for hours to say a last goodbye to their Lurleen.

15

For You

*I stand and watch her until at length she hangs like a
speck of white cloud just where the sea and sky come to
mingle with each other, then someone at my side says:
"There, she is gone." "Gone where?" Gone from my sight.
That is all. She is just as large in mast and hull and spar
as she was when she left my side.*

—Henry Van Dyke

In the winter and spring months of 1968, Mama never told me she was dying. There were no conversations about moving on without her. We never reminisced or recapitulated. We never talked about what she might want me to tell my children one day when they asked who she was and what kind of grandmother she would have been. Perhaps she had hope until the final moments of her life and was unable to accept her destiny. More likely, she didn't want to burden me as I was preparing to graduate from high school.

Mama did not live long enough to tell her own story. There were no diaries, no handwritten letters to us, no family movies, and only a few family photographs scattered about. The person that my mama was, and the person she could have become had she lived, will always elude me. The author Anita Smith described

"Peggy Sue, pinch me, I must be dreaming." May 3, 1966.

Mama as a "Lady of Courage" in her book *The Intimate Story of Lurleen Wallace: Her Crusade of Courage*. Ron Gibson, the book's editor, wrote in the introduction: "She rushed onto the stage of history only in time for a brief, if nonetheless memorable, performance before the lights went out. The audience applauded her dignity in the role in which she was cast—that of the protagonist of cancer. It is because the reader will come to know such a figure, tragic as her circumstance may finally have been, that this is not a sad book. It is a happy book."

Mama's deification through her suffering and death overshadowed her life. And for those who loved their Lady of Courage, there was no reason to defend her individual accomplishments as governor of Alabama, to investigate how her shortcomings made her who she was, or to set her free on the pages of history. To them, her nobility lay next to her in her grave.

The real story of Mama's life became irrelevant to history, and eventually even to our own family. We all too often circled the wagons to protect the memory of the Lady of Courage rather than celebrate who she was. I became accustomed to not looking beyond the stories that we always told, the ones with a punchline rather than those with depth.

Much of what we had been as a family died with Mama. There were no more vacations, Christmas lists, birthday cakes, or joyful moments. We didn't know how to do those things without her.

Back in Clayton, when I was young, Mama would sometimes come to visit the make-believe houses I would scratch out with a tree limb or broom handle on the dirt floor of our sagging garage. She helped make my floor plan more livable. She brought glasses of Kool-Aid for the two of us, and we would sit in metal yard chairs in my "living room."

"One day you will have a real house," she would say. "So when I come to visit be sure you have a room for me." I always promised I would.

In 1977, I moved into a real house of my own, and in June 1978, I brought Mama's grandson, Leigh Chancellor Kennedy, home to live in what would have been her room. Leigh's serene curiosity was unruffled and unafraid. His deep cerulean eyes seemed to look beyond me as if they were contemplating some universal truth.

A decade later, our son Morgan Burns Kennedy was born. His eyes narrowed when something went awry. His smiles were discreet. There was no doubt in my mind that Burns Kennedy had the "no monkey business around here" soul of Mamaw. He would have her "tell it like it is, ain't no use in sugarcoating it" personality.

In a moment of wishing that Mama could be there with me as I was rocking Burns in my arms, I began to think how things might have been different if she had declined to run for governor. Why would she have chosen politics over us when she had so little time? The nights and days she stood on a makeshift stage shaking hands with strangers were days and nights I was at home alone. I envied friends who shopped with their mother, went to a picture show, got their daddy to help them with their algebra.

When Burns became animated and restless in my arms and stared at me through squinting eyes, his hands balled up in boxer style, I wished I could call on Mamaw and Mama. I pulled him close to comfort him but he was comfortless. He was upset but not crying. "Are you about to pitch a fit?" I asked. "How I wish I could ask Mamaw and Mama what to do with you! But they left you and me a long time ago, so I guess it's just us."

Burns relaxed and with his eyes wide open looked straight into mine. It was as if he understood what I said but disagreed with my opinion. Then somewhere in my heart, I came to understand that all that Mama did, she had done for us. Lurleen Wallace was a woman of courage because of her life rather than a Lady of Courage because of her death.

I dream about standing in the shallows of the Alabama Gulf with Mama as she casts her rod toward the sky. The silver spinner catches the last light as it arcs up and over the water.

"Here, hold the rod for me for a second." Mama says as she cups her hand around a cigarette lighter to fend off a breeze. "Let's get lucky. What do you think?"

"Yep, let's get lucky," I reply with a smile.

"See that biggest ship heading through the pass?" she asks as she points toward the water. "Watch it now, as it heads out to sea. It will look like it's getting smaller and smaller, but it will always stay the same. That's because of the way we see it, not because of the way it really is."

"Are we like that ship?" I ask. "We are always the same, even if we are very far away and even when no one can see us?"

"I think we are."

My mother was reminding me that she would always be there with me in spirit. She would endure in my heart as the mother I loved. That would never change.

———

IN APRIL 1968, a few weeks before she died, Mama called me to her room. It was the night of the senior prom. "Turn around," she said as I walked through the door. "Mary Jo showed me the material she was going to use to make your dress. Come closer so I can see how lovely you are. Now turn around so I can see the back. Come sit by me. I have something for you."

Mama reached beneath the cover and retrieved a small gift box. "This is your graduation present, but I am so excited about all of this that I just can't wait that long, and I knew they would look so pretty with your dress. I can't wait to see them on you."

I took the pair of small diamond earrings from the box and put them on.

"Now, keep your hair pulled back so everyone can see them. Give me a kiss and go have some fun." Mama lay back on the pillow. "I want to hear all about it real soon."

I never got to tell Mama about that night. I sometimes wish I could have. Some years later, I took those earrings and had them mounted on either side of the diamond in my engagement ring to remind me of the night Mama said goodbye.

"This is where your grandmother walked . . ."
Me, Leigh, and Burns in Gulf Shores,
Alabama, 1990.

16

Stand Up

They're building a bridge over the Potomac for all the
white liberals fleeing to Virginia.

—George Wallace

L ate in the afternoon of Thursday, May 9, 1968, we returned
to the Governor's Mansion following Mama's funeral. Earlier
that day, thousands of Alabamians stood three and four deep
along the streets and boulevards on the route of Mama's funeral
cortege. Their love for Lurleen was palpable. Mama had directed
that these lines by Elizabeth Barrett Browning be read at her
funeral as an expression of her love for the people of Alabama:

I love you not only for what you are,
but for what I am when I am with you.
I love you not only for what you have made of yourself,
but for what you are making of me.
I love you for the part of me that you bring out.

The Governor's Mansion was veiled in sorrow as we drove through the gates. The house was reminiscent of a hotel ballroom following the last dance; no more music, just occasional rustlings as from petals dropping from dying roses or crepe paper streamers floating to the floor.

There was nothing there that could reassure me or comfort me. I wondered what it would feel like to soon be a guest in my mama's house, hesitant to climb the stairs or venture into my old bedroom. I felt the same way as I had many years before when I watched Daddy turn out the lights and lock the door behind us on the day we left Clayton for the last time.

Governor Albert Brewer, the former lieutenant governor and Mama's friend, offered to allow us sufficient time to regain our composure and collect ourselves before moving out. Daddy declined his offer. And we did have a home to go to where the remnants of Mama's last bits of her fleeting life resided. Whether it was Mama's sense of the inevitable outcome of her illness, or her desire to have the home she always dreamed of after she was out of office, she and Daddy had purchased a rambling ranch-style house in one of Montgomery's newest housing developments, across the street from our church and in a neighborhood filled with acquaintances and friends. During the summer and fall of 1967, Mama spent as much of her time at that house as her cancer and her work obligations allowed. She left that house behind for us to live in.

"Not a place to cry in," I could hear her telling me. "Lord knows we've done enough of that in our lives. I've worked hard to get you all set up, everything I could think of. And every once in a while, I want you to remember that we finally made it. No more holes in your shoes, Peggy Sue. Just come on in and sit with me and have a Coke or a cup of coffee." And with a smile veiled in smoke from her Benson & Hedges cigarette: "Guess our ship finally came in."

Daddy's determination to make a swift departure from the mansion was not to accommodate Governor Brewer; it was due to the unraveling of his ability to keep himself pulled together. His stiff upper lip was about to crumple. As soon as the last moving van pulled away from our new home and the security guards retreated to a small office on the other side of the rear driveway, Daddy wandered from room to room. He then collapsed on the den sofa. With his shoes still on and a thin black tie knotted neatly beneath the collar of his short-sleeved white dress shirt, Daddy turned his face to the wall. His sorrow was mixed with a healthy dose of regret. He cried for hours without stopping and refused to pull himself together during brief moments between waves of anguish, indifferent to the way the rest of us felt.

After several days, my attempted words of comfort turned to anger as I demanded that he get up and take care of us. If visitors were allowed or family members stopped by, he managed to sit up for a conversation or usher them to a small and dingy wood-paneled room chock-full of wooden plaques and framed awards. These mementos climbed all four walls and spilled out over the linoleum floor.

Several weeks after Mama's funeral, Daddy called Governor Brewer and invited him to come to the house for a visit. He wanted to talk to Brewer about the rumor that Daddy planned to run for governor in 1970. Daddy promised Brewer that there would be no Wallace on the ballot in two years. He reminisced about Mama's affection for Brewer and his wife. Upon over-hearing Daddy's promise that he would not challenge Brewer in the next election, I was relieved that we would remain in the house that Mama had prepared for us. Her presence was strong there—it was where she had wanted us to be. Finally there would be some stability in our lives—a place to build a life.

AFTER SPENDING MORE than a month in seclusion, Daddy turned his attention back to his presidential campaign. The campaign staff breathed a collective sigh of relief. There were no stand-ins who could incite the rabid enthusiasm Daddy inspired, replicate the Wallace bravado, or whip the rising tide of discon-tent amid forlorn and forgotten working-class whites who were the engine of "Stand Up for America."

Without an established political party or a stable of wealthy donors to fuel a national advertising campaign on behalf of the American Independent Party, Daddy became more than a polit-ical party's standard-bearer—his character and personality became the message itself.

It's worth noting that while Daddy had not created the American Independent Party, it hadn't existed in the way it did after he decided to run as an Independent. Previously, the AIP had been on the ballot in a very limited number of states. Daddy and his campaign were able to get it on the ballot in every state in the union—a feat that was to recast American politics in the later part of the twentieth century. He was able to say: "I am running as an independent because there's not a dime's bit of difference between the Republican and Democratic parties and neither of them represents the values of the people I represent." Those people were overwhelmingly comprised of the white working class who felt the rest of the country didn't give a damn about them. Through Daddy's efforts, they now had a national party of their own. Their grandchildren would one day be voting for Trump.

Daddy had no illusions he would win the presidency, but through the reach of the AIP he had positioned himself as a power broker and defined an electorate that today holds the levers of power. No one thought he could pull it off. But he did, and it was shocking—much like Trump's victory in 2016.

EVEN AFTER A monthlong absence from politics, Daddy's poll numbers were holding steady. They would climb as white working-class Americans felt cast into bubbling pots of fear and discontent. An incendiary mix of hatred and grief roamed the streets of American cities following the assassinations of Martin Luther King Jr. and Robert Kennedy. The month of May was the bloodiest month of the Vietnam War: 2,415 American soldiers killed. Antiwar protesters marched on college campuses. On May 12, the first African American demonstrators arrived at the National Mall in Washington to occupy Resurrection City as part of the Poor People's Campaign led by Rev. Ralph Abernathy.

America the Beautiful was coming apart at the seams. Down-and-out white folks who had worked all their lives, gone to church on Sundays, never asked for a handout, and still took their hats off when the flag went by were furious. Their response to the protests and calls for change? *America, love it or leave it.* To this constituency Daddy was no longer just another presidential candidate with the right ideas, he was a part of their family: someone who talked the way they talked, looked the way they looked, and thought the way they thought. The very things about Daddy that reporters made fun of and scoffed at endeared him to his supporters. Daddy's affinity for custom suits, expensive cigars, and manicures were offset by his habit of spitting into a handkerchief, the ever-present cigar in his mouth, and the sheen of his Brylcreemed hair. His countrified, bombastic, and in-your-face manner gave him an authenticity that politicians often lack.

The Stand Up for America campaign moved from town to town like a national county fair with hawkers, barkers, and bevies of Southern belles, personified by one of Alabama's own traveling music duos, the Mona Lisa Singers.

Mona Taylor and her sister Lisa were daughters of a wealthy but eccentric coal mine operator from northwest Alabama. Several archival films of Wallace rallies catch the two singers belting out catchy tunes as they sway beneath petticoats, beating tambourines on their thighs. I didn't know it at the time, but Lynda Lee "Lisa" Taylor was head over her high heels for George Wallace. If I had known she would one day become my stepmother, I might have introduced myself!

BY THE MIDDLE of June, Daddy's populist message was gaining more traction. The anti-Wallace backlash intensified—he was a fascistic redneck racist from a backward state with backward ideas. The Wallace caravan moved from city to city. It had homespun humor and young girls prancing up and down the aisles with plastic donation buckets. It also had Wallace supporters with baseball bats. They were there to quell the rising tide of shouted invective and flying objects that were hurled at the stage. Chair-throwing, fist-fighting, stage-rushing, and arrests had become part of the anti-Wallace campaign culture. When chaos erupted at Wallace rallies, before he was rushed off the stage by his security detail, Daddy would stand behind his lectern and observe the scene with an almost serene expression.

In late June, I began traveling with Daddy's campaign. For me, it was a reprieve from my overwhelming sadness over Mama's death. Daddy and I would sit together in the first row of seats on the campaign plane. His white-knuckle fear of flying always kept him buckled up; he would lean back with his braced feet planted halfway up the galley wall in front of us. The campaign crew seldom approached us, and for the most part we sat in silence as he stared out the window. Attempts to reminisce about Mama or talk about the past fell flat. He was lost in his own thoughts.

ON JULY 26, Daddy's plane departed from Montgomery early in the morning on a flight to Providence, Rhode Island. The aircraft was filled with staff members, reporters, and lots of female Wallace volunteers. A small crowd of respectful anti-Wallace protesters greeted our limousine in the parking lot of the down-town Sheraton hotel. Daddy made it a point to shake hands with each one. The scheduled rally that night was to be held at a Shriners hall on the outskirts of town.

The crowd was large and anxious. Protesters unrolled banners and began to chant as Daddy rose to speak. He taunted them and their rage with impertinent remarks, telling them, "All you hippies and pseudo-intellectuals are going to be through come election day. You use all those nasty four-letter words when you are talking about us. Well, how about these two for you, *work* and *soap*." Pointing to a male protester in the crowd, he would say, "You're a pretty little thing"—then, after a pause—"Oh, my goodness, you're a he, not a she." And the crowds would roar.

Amid shouts of anger and roars of approval, fights broke out from one end of the hall to the other. Several protesters rushed the stage. Incensed women joined in the melee. Daddy's voice rose above the crowd with more taunts, advising that the next anarchist that lay down in front of his car would find it the last one they ever lay down in front of. Eventually, the police gained the upper hand and the protesters were driven out of the hall.

After the rally, security guards helped me escape from an angry mob congregated behind the stage and outside. I was lifted up and over grabbing hands as obscenities were shouted at me. As I sat shivering in the back of the limousine, I noticed that the dress Mama had given me for my birthday was covered with black spray paint and ink marks. A woman came up to the car and began beating on my window with a leg from a metal folding chair. Then she was gone, fallen back and away into the crowds of fury. I've sometimes wondered what she would have done to me if I had rolled down the window.

IN LATE JUNE, I had applied for admission to Mississippi State College for Women. My MSCW application had been submitted

On campus at Mississippi State College for Women,
October 27, 1968.

well past the application deadline. I worried that my high school grades, high school activities, and tardiness would doom me. But what I did not know was that the MSCW president, William Hogarth, was an avowed segregationist. While many presidents of colleges and universities throughout the South had accepted integration, there weren't going to be any red carpets, welcoming teas, or happy smiles awaiting African Americans at MSCW as long as Dr. Hogarth was in charge. As the daughter of America's perhaps most prominent and influential segregationist, my application was quickly approved. At the time, I had no idea why I had been so eagerly admitted.

On the drive to Columbus, I took a detour to Knoxville to see Mamaw and Mr. Henry. Mamaw stepped through the screen door as I rolled to a stop. "I told Henry that I hoped you would stop by on your way to Mississippi," Mamaw said, hugging me. "I don't have anything cooked up for you to take along, but come up in the house and I'll find something to feed you. Tell me how things are back home. Your daddy is gallivantin', I see. Guess you might be movin' to the White House. I hope he at least gives you some walkin'-around money to have in your purse for little extras."

Mamaw's chatter continued. I sat at the kitchen table and chased half a ham sandwich with a jelly glass of iced tea. Mr. Henry stuck his head in the front door and waved before disappearing around the side of the house. Mamaw and I walked on the rim of our collective sadness. We knew that if we started crying about Mama we wouldn't be able to stop.

Mamaw's bitterness about Mama's death had given way to acceptance of the circumstances of our lives. Mamaw and Mr. Henry were too exhausted to look over their shoulder and wonder why.

A SECRET SERVICE agent was waiting for me as I drove up to the front of my dorm. Because of my frequent travel with Daddy's campaign, Daddy requested that an agent be assigned to me through the November election. I still remember what it felt like to watch mothers and daughters climb out of cars while fathers opened trunks filled with suitcases of clothes and boxes of keepsakes and mementos. Although I did the best I could, my dorm room lacked the cheeriness of a mother's touch. There were no packing boxes to arrive later, no curtains on the windows, only the eager faces of new friends stopping by to ask if my daddy was really George Wallace.

Eventually, my dormmates grew weary of my perpetual sadness when there was just so much to be happy about being away from home, not to mention the glamorous life I was leading. Driving a new Ford Mustang with a handsome Secret Service agent following behind, picture-taking and interviews, and boarding private planes on the weekends to campaign with a famous father was just more than anyone could ever dream of. But this hollow glamour and pretentious rigmarole just made me miss my mama more. I would have traded it all in a heartbeat for the sound of her voice and her warm embrace.

Dr. Hogarth and his administration viewed me as a feather in his cap amid the pervasive racist culture of MSCW, but in the eyes of many African American students, I stood as a living, breathing symbol of American apartheid.

In the fall of 1968, I was neither white nor black. The color of my skin was Wallace.

17

Things Just Change

*Death is not the greatest loss in life. The greatest loss is
what dies inside us while we live.*

—Norman Cousins

While Daddy may have been disappointed at the outcome
of his 1968 presidential campaign, there was no doubt in
the minds of political pundits that George Wallace was a man to
be reckoned with.

The American Independent Party and George Wallace hit a
home run with white middle-class voters, and so it seemed time
for the Democratic and Republican parties, or at least for the one
that wanted to win, to make a sharp right turn not just in the South
but all across the country before the next national election.

Daddy returned to Alabama with legions of angry American
voters in his pocket and an Alabama electorate whose Southern
pride had been inflamed. To many Alabamians, Daddy's success
across the nation was not just about him—it was about the

Southern culture of disaffection: the "those other folks think they are better than us" mentality. Daddy was a symbol of "We showed them, now, didn't we."

But in Alabama, a man's word was still his bond, and Daddy's promise to Governor Brewer not to run against him in 1970 was going to be hard to break, even for the most ardent Wallace supporters. Governor Brewer was popular among both white and black Alabamians and had gained the respect and allegiance of more than a few of Daddy's advisers, county coordinators, and local politicians who still believed "a promise is a promise."

Four years out of politics was not something Daddy could abide, though. The notion of having more time to spend with his family, take vacations, join the PTA, or settle down and practice law no doubt made his knees buckle. He had either been campaigning for something or dreaming about it for his entire life.

To him, running for governor again was less about breaking a promise than about "Albert Brewer should have known better in the first place. He caught me at a weak moment, out of my mind with grief." Daddy could justify anything. This tendency assuaged whatever pangs of conscience he may have had at the schoolhouse door and his role around the incidents on the Edmund Pettus Bridge. Reneging on a promise to Albert Brewer would not even come close to the moral flexibility he demonstrated on other occasions.

Daddy wanted his job back. While it may have been difficult for his former employees, friends, and supporters who had taken him at his word and signed on with the Brewer campaign to decide what they should do, it was not difficult for him. He wanted what he wanted, and he was going to get it.

By the fall of 1969, the Wallace loyalists were energized, finding vacant buildings on county courthouse squares, looking for flatbed trailers, and rigging up sound trucks for the coming campaign. The fact that there were "Wallace traitors" lurking around merely fired up the engines of the second generation of Wallace supporters. There was no way they were going to take the picture of Governor George and Lurleen off the wall, much less turn redcoat on them. Albert Brewer may have been doing a good job, but he was no "fightin' little judge." Nevertheless, the Brewer coalition of industrialists and businesspeople, middle- and upper-class whites, and African Americans was formidable. And then there was Richard Nixon.

In early 1970, the White House was seeing polls showing that in a three-man presidential race in 1972 between Nixon, Humphrey, and the Independent candidate Wallace, Nixon held a 54 percent advantage. Without Wallace running as an Independent, Nixon climbed to 76 percent. Projections indicated that once Wallace announced, the American Independent Party would gain momentum and the president's numbers would fall on the short side of 50 percent. George Wallace could be a great threat to Nixon's legacy—that is, if Daddy was reelected governor in 1970.

On March 10, 1970, Postmaster General Winton Blount, one of the wealthiest men in Alabama, traveled to the White House to meet with President Nixon and his aide John Ehrlichman to discuss the Alabama primary election. According to the polls, Brewer was up by nineteen points, and the *Washington Post* reported that the Wallace numbers were sinking with working-class whites.

If Daddy lost the Democratic primary, his whole campaign infrastructure would collapse along with his national reputation. Daddy might still own the Cadillac, but the wheels and engine would be gone. And when that happened, the most significant risk to Nixon's being elected to a second term would be eliminated.

Several days later, one of Nixon's attorneys removed $100,000 in hundred-dollar bills from a Nixon-controlled safe-deposit box at a branch of the Chase Manhattan Bank in New York and carried it to the lobby of the Sherry-Netherland hotel near Central Park. Following the exchange of a coded message, he handed the money to a Brewer representative and walked out. Nixon authorized two additional drops, an additional $200,000 at the Sherry-Netherland and $100,000 at the Beverly Wilshire in Beverly Hills—all in all, $400,000 in crisp hundred-dollar bills to the Brewer campaign.

In addition, Nixon directed the IRS to comb through every tax return, bank record, sales slip, and property record of Daddy's and the dealings between Daddy and Uncle Gerald. In early April, the IRS report was leaked to the *Washington Post*, and on April 13, Jack Anderson's "Washington Merry-Go-Round" column, which was syndicated in more than three hundred newspapers, alleged that Uncle Gerald and others were being investigated by the IRS for illegal kickbacks and violations of campaign financing laws. With only three weeks to go before the primary election, Anderson's article reappeared in most of the Alabama daily newspapers.

The information appeared to be devastating. But Daddy proclaimed that the Brewer campaign had ganged up with the

Washington hotshots to swing the election Brewer's way, as if Alabama voters were too ignorant to make up their own minds. Daddy rolled through the Alabama countryside with stops at every crossroad, courthouse, and café he could find. Finally, it was something to build on, even as his poll numbers had continued to slide.

On May 5, election day, Governor Brewer led the pack of candidates in the Democratic primary. Daddy's onslaught of accusations and declarations gave him enough traction to come in second with a vote spread of twelve thousand. With the Wallace vote and the cumulative votes of the other five candidates, Brewer was the clear front-runner, but he failed to gain a majority of the total votes. There was going to be a runoff.

Being a student of the electoral history of Alabama, Daddy was aware that there had never been a second-place candidate in a Democratic primary who had gone on to win a runoff. While he had enjoyed making many historic moments, some better than others, in his lifetime, Daddy became convinced that fate had finally found him.

Daddy checked into a motel in Birmingham, locked the door, pulled down the shades, turned out the light, and took to the bed. His life was over. He had been denied the one thing he loved the most—winning. Of course, he loved his children on sunny days, but the voters pulled the wrong rabbit out of the hat and his children should be as upset as he was about their doomed existence.

Uncle Gerald, along with a close friend from Clayton, Jere Beasley, who was facing a runoff in the lieutenant governor's race that same year, was shocked at Daddy's condition when they entered his lights-out-and-curtains-drawn motel room. After their encouragement and sympathy failed to gain a foothold and "What about your family?" had no effect, shaming him with a dose of "You owe it to all those people who worked day and night to get you this far" at least got the pillow off his head.

By the time they got to the outskirts of Birmingham, Daddy's heartbreak had become "Albert Brewer has no idea what is about to hit him." Burning ashes from his lit cigar rushed through his rolled-down window as, reinvigorated, he plunged back into the throng.

The 1970 primary runoff, a testament to Daddy's "comeback kid" luck, will go down as the most virulent and hate-filled election in the history of Alabama, and up to that time in America. The Wallace faithful fanned out to beat bushes and shake trees in every county, registering more than thirty thousand new voters over the course of one and a half weeks. Cars full of volunteers followed trucks full of Wallace yard signs and staked them out on main roads, county roads, and dirt roads.

Seeing the devastating effect of the battalions of automobiles loaned out to the Wallace campaign, filled with signs, smear sheets, and spiteful people speeding along gravel roads and black-tops like an army of foraging locusts, the Brewer campaign approached the owner of a large automobile dealership, where most of the Wallace campaign cars were coming from, and offered to pay $100,000 if he would call the cars in. The offer was declined.

As for the IRS investigation of the Wallaces, it was abandoned in January 1972, one day before Daddy's announcement that he would run for president as a Democrat. His decision came with no advance warning. Uncle Gerald attributed Daddy's startling and sudden decision to abandon the American Independent Party to an agreement between Daddy and President Nixon. In exchange for ending all federal investigations of the Wallaces, Daddy would run as a Democrat—a deal that Uncle Gerald would have benefited from.

Thousands of American Independent Party members across the United States were gearing up and recruiting local and state-wide candidates in their home states to run on the ticket with George Wallace. They had no forewarning. Many became disillusioned, while others moved forward alone.

Daddy won the Democratic primary runoff and would go on to easily win the general election in November. We were going to live again in the Governor's Mansion on South Perry Street.

DADDY MADE HISTORY with his 1970 win. On January 4, 1971, he married Cornelia Snively, the niece of one of Alabama's most colorful governors, Wallace friend "Big" Jim Folsom, at a Presbyterian church not far from the Governor's Mansion. I was happy for them. The thought of having Cornelia living in the mansion was exciting.

Although Uncle Gerald and other Wallace insiders had suggested to Cornelia that she marry Daddy after his inauguration, she would have no part of it. She was going to be Alabama's newest First Lady as soon as Daddy said, "So help me, God," on his inaugural day. That was Cornelia's first mistake on the road to her undoing. There had never been a spot in the Wallace Machine for the kind of engaged First Lady that Cornelia wanted to be.

Cornelia was a powerful presence—the kind of woman that people turn their heads to stare at when she walks into a room. She was strong-willed, aggressive, and had a penchant for drama. She was lovely and charismatic: tanned skin, dark hair worn like Loretta Lynn's, straight and combed back in front, cascading curls in back, and beautiful, flashing eyes.

CORNELIA MADE A strong impression, but it paled beside that of her mother, Ruby. Ruby and her husband, Dr. Austin, lived in a stately but somewhat run-down house not far from the Governor's Mansion on the edge of Old Cloverdale, one of Montgomery's most prestigious neighborhoods.

I could not believe what I was seeing when we first went to their house for dinner. They had returned from a medical convention only a few hours before we arrived, and it was apparent that neither of them had time to freshen up—much less sober up. Dr. Austin had lost his shoes and Ruby's green satin cocktail dress had a large rip on the right shoulder, as did one of her matching lime-green fishnet stockings.

"Well, hell. We came up the hard way," Ruby said, explaining her dishevelment. "Hard drinking, hard partying, and hard living."

The elegantly dressed Cornelia navigated the treacherous waters of Ruby's unpredictable behavior with as much dignity as she could muster. Daddy, for a change, seemed to be without words. I sat there trying not to stare.

"See this bell?" Ruby picked up a small crystal bell from beside her plate. "Cornelia tells me I can't just yell back to the kitchen when we run out of something. I got to ring this damn bell."

Holding the bell over her head, Ruby began to wave it back and forth as if she was about to throw it across the room. Ruby's maid, with a look of exasperation on her face, came through the kitchen's swinging door.

"Well, hell," Ruby announced. "It works!"

IN CORNELIA WALLACE'S mind, the marriage between the House of Folsom and the House of Wallace was going to usher in a new golden age in the Heart of Dixie.

Me and Daddy at my twenty-first birthday party,
January 24, 1971.

On January 24, three days after the inauguration, Daddy and Cornelia hosted their first private event at the mansion. The dining room was decorated with bouquets of carnations and sterling silver candelabra from the battleship USS *Alabama* that ran the length of the dark mahogany table. Following dinner, Daddy stood and proposed a toast to me on the occasion of my twenty-first birthday. Daddy and I stood on the grand staircase in the entry hall for photos. Looking up, I could see the door to Mama's bedroom and the sofa where we once sat. I was back in the place where we once lived, but it would never again be home. Perhaps, I thought, I could still find happiness there—I knew without a doubt that that's what Mama would have wanted.

18

Buckle My Shoes

Love is big. Love can hold anger, love can hold pain, love can even hold hatred. It's all about love.

—*Alice Walker*

C ornelia offered a fresh start to our newly minted First Family. She was the opposite of the adage "Women should be seen but not heard." Although Daddy's territorial inner circle worried that she would have too much influence on his politics, at first, at least, she showed no interest in policy matters and began fussing with his appearance and wardrobe. His natty black suits, white short-sleeved cotton shirts, and pencil-thin ties became polyester blends of rainbow colors and paisley. While the fashion of the seventies was not one of the best moments in American couture, Daddy's makeover made him well dressed for the times.

Cornelia soon became a woman of influence, not necessarily in the public's eye, but in Daddy's mind. But rather than creating alliances with the Wallace old hats, she challenged them and on occasion countermanded them. Cornelia's affinity for whispering in Daddy's ear on matters of politics was deemed treasonous by his cronies and no doubt by a large number of Daddy's female admirers who would gladly have given much more than their eyeteeth had he chosen them.

While Mama may have offered advice, she posed no threat to the Wallace brain trust, and when she became governor, they became her brain trust. "This new wife is certainly no Lurleen" became a common thread of conversation around the coffee pots and water coolers in the governor's office.

Cornelia was ambitious and saw herself as an equal partner in Daddy's destiny. She was proud to be called the "Jackie Kennedy of the rednecks." Daddy's inner circle viewed Cornelia as a threat, and Cornelia viewed them as a threat to her stature as Daddy's wife. The old-time crowd of Wallace lieutenants, moneymakers, and confidants assumed they had an open invitation to drop by the mansion "at will." Cornelia quickly disabused them of this notion. They learned that Governor Big Jim Folsom's open invitation of "Y'all Come" had not been passed down to his niece. While Daddy ran the state, Cornelia was going to run their ample social life. The state buzzed with "I told you so's" following an early 1973 broadcast of the Dick Cavett show live from the Governor's Mansion. Even Dick Cavett looked startled when Cornelia batted her eyes, smiled, and said, "I like to travel so fast they had to put a governor on me." That was Cornelia in a nutshell.

———

FOLLOWING DADDY'S INAUGURATION, I moved into the guest-house at the rear of the mansion. It provided me with privacy but was less than twenty feet from the kitchen door. A parking pad separated the two buildings. During the week, I drove a daily commute of one hour each way to Troy State University, where I was majoring in special education.

I wanted to be close to Daddy and enjoyed Cornelia's company. Her strong-willed nature and claims to be always right (including her absolute conviction that there were UFOs circling the planet) was a small price to pay for her usual good humor and mostly good intentions. Cornelia was a breath of fresh air that seemed to

Me as Alabama's Cherry Blossom Princess in Washington D.C.'s Cherry Blossom Festival, April 8, 1972.

chase away the ghosts of heartache that lived at the core of our family.

Big Ruby was a frequent visitor to the mansion. While Ruby was unpredictable when she was sober, she was predictably out of control when she was on a binge. She was generally a crowd pleaser at local bars and nefarious hangouts, but she had been banned from one establishment after being escorted there by a pet monkey that began throwing items at other bar patrons. Following their removal, the contrite bar owner phoned Daddy. "Governor, I hate that you had to send someone over here to take care of this situation. Ruby is really good for business, and she has always been welcome. But the monkey has got to go."

On January 13, 1972, Daddy announced he was running for president as a Democrat, joining a crowded field of eleven other candidates. It was the kind of mash-up that Daddy enjoyed. Divide and conquer was his specialty. As his new and improved campaign geared up, his fundraising numbers were impressive, the campaign staff was experienced, and Daddy's appearance and dress were overhauled, Southern-style.

Light-colored double-knit suits were lucky to have three wearings before the front of the pants legs were pockmarked with melt holes caused by hot ashes from Daddy's cigar. There was a closetful of replacements. Buckle shoes replaced shoestrings, and wide ties—paisley, of course—eliminated the need for a napkin tuck at mealtimes to help keep his shirt free of splatters.

The Wallace campaign was a juggernaut. On March 14, record numbers of Floridians turned out to vote in the Democratic primary. Not only did Daddy win the primary, he carried every county in the state. Daddy was a viable candidate, and he was on his way to be at least a kingmaker at a brokered convention, perhaps a vice presidential running mate or even a nominee.

While a few political highbrows acknowledged that Daddy might have a chance, others said "this just can't happen in America." But tell that to shouting crowds of angry and dispossessed voters, and they would tell you to go to hell. Daddy understood the power of hate and fear and exploited these feelings to gather support.

Daddy's politics was more than just bombastic style. The establishment and other politicians viewed him as a demagogue. Nobody will buy what he is selling, they declared. Just take a look at him. Take him out of those Alabama backwoods and he'll be finished. That was a mistake. And forty-eight years later, disaffected voters responded similarly to Trump. They rebelled against the same intellectualism and paternalism that Daddy railed against.

Daddy tapped into a complicated network of political ideals and cultural values. He was aware of the somewhat perverse attitude of the white middle class toward power. He understood that when middle-class whites perceived that the American Dream was no longer within reach, they would become blindly loyal to the person they believed could reclaim it for them. In 1972 and again in 2016, white working-class Americans needed to feel vindicated. No more handouts or political favors to the elites, no illegal immigrants stealing our jobs, stand up when the flag goes by, anger and fear are justified—get real! Stand Up for America. Make America Great Again.

Daddy and Donald Trump would have agreed on at least one thing. While powerless people may sometimes be skeptical of those who have the power, powerful people are the ones they most often worship, accepting their authority without question and teaching their children that respect for authority is a moral absolute. And that is at the heart of the appeal of both "Stand Up for America" and "Make America Great Again."

Daddy's strategy of articulating and mobilizing the grievances of the dispossessed would become one of the core strategies of the Trump campaign forty-four years later. It was the politics of rage and fear. It was resentment for no particular reason. It was a tent revival in the dead of summer, slapping mosquitoes and singing "Amazing Grace" while the preacher was fooling around out back.

On March 13, 1972, the *New York Times* published an article written by the reporter James T. Wooten that focused on the psychological and political culture of the Wallace campaign. Using a Wallace rally the day before in Orlando as the context, Wooten described the essential elements of the brew of patriotism, evangelism, political poetry, imagery, a dash of fear, and a bit of hate that made a George Wallace rally so powerful. The article was entitled "Wallace's Rallies Blend Evangelism, Music and Salesmanship."

> Mr. Wallace's Florida campaign, which has consistently outdrawn those of the other 11 candidates, moves by day from one town to the next in cars and campers, station wagons and jet planes—but the thrust of all of its energies is inevitably pointed to The Rally.
>
> These rallies for Governor Wallace, who has forged a career out of Southern segregation and states' rights, are

a mix of old-time rural evangelism, slick country-music salesmanship and tried and true.

The Baptist preacher is George Mangum, a 38-year-old minister who has a parish near Selma, Ala., and has worked in Wallace campaigns since 1966. His huge shock of gray hair and his deep, booming voice are enough to attract the initial attention of those who attend the Wallace rallies. Throughout the affairs, he raises his hands above his head, whirling them energetically, calling for applause, and the people consistently respond.

The religious emphasis of the campaign was never more clearly characterized than in the opening prayer at last night's rally here. "May every head be bowed as we begin a spiritual conversation with our God about some of the political problems in our country," the Rev. John Book, also a Baptist clergyman, prayed. "We give you thanksgiving, O Lord, for men of courage like George Wallace."

GRAMMER ON GUITAR

From the prayer, the rally moves quickly to the music of Billy Grammer, a veteran country music star from the Grand Ole Opry in Nashville who is a fixture on the Wallace campaign trail this year. Although he is frequently joined on the stage by other stars, such as Hank Snow, Ferlin Husky, and Grandpa Jones, it is Mr. Grammer whose skill with the guitar and whose broad repertoire of country songs pleases the people night after night. Like many of the other country musicians who have appeared at Wallace rallies, Mr. Grammer seems committed to the Wallace campaign. "I don't mind anybody knowing how I feel," the 46-year-old native of Southern Illinois told the crowd last night. "I think a whole lot of things are basically wrong with this country and I think that a lot of them can be cured by a good Christian man like George Wallace being in the White House."

The rural-church emphasis continues into the middle portion of the rally when Mr. Mangum begins his appeal for campaign funds. As he speaks, young girls with plastic buckets circulate throughout the audience accepting anonymous donations, and when the collection is finished Mr. Mangum continues to exhort the people to sign fundraising petitions.

Meanwhile, in the lobby at every stop, a team of Wallace staff men hawk various souvenirs of the campaign including bumper stickers, lapel pins, and a caricature watch.

It is not known how much money is collected at these rallies. The Wallace campaign has been asked to provide that information but has not.

The people who come to Wallace rallies seem to share a complete disaffection with government at all levels. They are white, blue-collar families. They are old, and they are young, and throughout the evening they show little hesitance about expressing the anger they feel toward the "bureaucrats, hypocrites and uninterested politicians" whom Mr. Wallace castigates in his speech.

"Give it to them, George," they frequently yell. "That's right, George," comes the call. "We love George," another woman screams.

On the stage, amid the clutter and disarray of camera and sound equipment, four Alabama state troopers stand stolidly at either end, peering intently into the crowd. Their watch seems unnecessary, for throughout the campaign Mr. Wallace has spoken only to sympathetic audiences and has been interrupted three times by hecklers, who were quickly silenced and soon left.

When the speech is finished, Mr. Wallace moves, rather hesitantly at first, to the edge of the stage where the people often flock, their hands raised and stretched toward the candidate.

CUFFLINKS DISAPPEAR

"Glad to see you, glad to see you," he chants as he moves down the chain of hands, a state trooper moving behind him and holding to his belt. As is the case with many other politicians, cufflinks are often missing after the round of handshakes.

"It seems to me that these rallies ought to tell this country and you newsmen in particular something important," Mr. Wallace said last week. "If I'm getting all these people out every night, and the other candidates are having to struggle to draw a crowd at all, doesn't that say something about the truth of what I'm telling these folks?"

Whether that thesis is true or not, The Rally is indeed important to Mr. Wallace. It seems to underscore the confidence that he and his supporters have in the outcome of Tuesday's voting.

"If he doesn't win," a middle-aged woman wearing at least 17 Wallace buttons across her bodice said last night after The Rally, "there's not a cow in Texas."

"Your daddy is back in the dining room eating his breakfast," Mary, the cook, said as I walked through the mansion's back door and stepped into the restaurant-sized kitchen. "What you want to eat this morning?" she asked.

"The usual," I replied.

"You traveling with your daddy today, or do you have school?"

"School," I replied. "Mondays are one of my long days. My last class doesn't start until four."

"Well, today is May 15. At least you don't have much more time before you get through. Go on in there and sit with your daddy. I'll bring your breakfast right out."

After eating, I gave Daddy a kiss on my way out of the dining room. "What time will y'all be home?" I asked.

"Won't be late," he replied. "They're already saying we are going to win Maryland and Michigan tomorrow."

Daddy looked at his watch and rang the buzzer for the kitchen. "Go tell Cornelia I'm leaving in a few minutes with or without her."

"You have a good day, be careful on that road," Mary said as I passed back through the kitchen. "You want a little something to take with you for a snack?'

"I'm fine," I replied.

"Well, I'll have something real nice for supper tonight when all y'all get back home."

Daddy's car was parked close by, with the engine running. "Have a safe trip," I said to the driver as I walked down the back steps of the mansion.

"We will," he replied. "You have a good day. It's supposed to be beautiful weather all the way up and back."

I was standing in the front room of the guesthouse when I heard the kitchen door open.

"Let's go," Daddy said.

I could hear the sound of his footsteps as he hurried down the stairs.

19

The Book of Lamentations

The events of our lives happen in a sequence in time, but in their significance to ourselves they find their own order . . . the continuous thread of revelation.

—Eudora Welty

I glanced at my watch. I was going to be early for my three o'clock class. I stood by the window on the second floor of the education building, not far from my classroom door. I was thinking about what I was going to wear the following day for the election returns rally in Montgomery. No doubt Daddy's grumbling attitude about his quick trip would turn to immodest smiles if he won the primaries in Maryland and Michigan the following day.

"I'm surprised to see you here!" said one of my classmates, walking toward me.

"I got here early," I replied.

Her eyes grew wide as she lifted her hand to her mouth. "You don't know, do you?" Her face was pale, and her voice sounded breathless as if she had been running.

An overwhelming sense of clarity seemed to surround me. I was hyperaware of the way the sunlight was coming through a window, the distant sound of a truck straining as it climbed a hill, a door slamming followed by a fever of loud voices.

"Know what?"

"Your daddy has been shot." She began to cry.

Was it relief that I felt? That what I knew was eventually going to happen had in fact had happened? The day Mama had paced when Daddy had made his stand in the schoolhouse door was the first time I had felt fear about his safety, but that fear had been there on and off from that day until the day he was struck down.

A professor ran toward me, gathered me up, and took me to the university president's office. Ralph Adams and his wife, Dorothy, were both stoic in the face of the news reports on the shooting.

"First Lurleen and now this," Dorothy said as she took me in her arms. "I have no words to say." Benita Sanders, a friend of mine, drove me back to Montgomery.

The radio blared in her car as we careened along the road, flashing the lights to make cars move over. Whipping wind from open windows helped keep nausea at bay. The street in front of the mansion was impassable. News trucks with blaring horns scattered people gathering on the sidewalks and in the street. Police cars with flashing lights blocked the mansion gates.

"This is still my house!" I shouted as I opened the passenger door and began to run. "This is still my house!"

Cornelia's secretary was standing under the portico. She grabbed me by the shoulders. "Listen to me," she said. "Your daddy is not dead. He is at a hospital in surgery. He is going to pull through this."

I stared at her with blank eyes.

"There is a plane waiting at the airport. Go get what you need."

THERE WAS LITTLE to be said as the plane took off and headed north. Daddy's physician avoided conjecture about Daddy's condition. "Let's just wait until we get there before we jump to any conclusions. He is alive and in good hands. That's all we need to know right now."

We had learned that an Alabama state trooper on Daddy's detail, a Secret Service agent, and a local Wallace supporter were also wounded in the attack. The troopers assigned to Daddy's detail were like members of our family, and E. C. Dothard was no exception. His wife was on the flight with us.

As we were boarding the plane in Montgomery, Ruby roared into the parking space in front of the aircraft hangar. With an oversized purse in one hand and a small suitcase in the other, Ruby began running toward the plane.

"She is not getting on this plane," one of Daddy's security guards said. "How do I close this door?" Even Ruby's screaming was no match for the mounting noise of the jet's turbines. "God help us when she does get there," the trooper said. Even in the midst of agony, we were briefly consumed with laughter.

IT WAS LESS than six hours between the time I found out about the shooting and our arrival in Maryland. Holy Cross Hospital was bathed in garish light as we approached it by way of a residential street. The front yards of upscale houses had become haphazard parking lots for media trucks and cars. People crowded the streets. Oversized media trucks clawed through the hospital's front lawn. A statue of the Virgin Mary, bathed in soft light, was surrounded by chaos.

Our cars were besieged when we arrived at the hospital entrance. Even the Secret Service could not keep the cameras at a distance. Cornelia was waiting for us in a private room on the surgical floor. Other than scattered bloodstains on the hem of her yellow dress, there was nothing else to suggest the horror of that day. Her composure and calm demeanor were a welcome respite.

"He is still in surgery, but he is holding his own," she said. Just after three in the morning we were allowed to see him. The doctors were guarded in their conversations. "Thankfully your father was in excellent health. Otherwise, he would have never reached the hospital. It is too soon to give you a prognosis. We are optimistic, but he needs assurances from all of you that he is going to get through this. You need to go see him."

The large surgical recovery room was obviously meant to accommodate more than one patient at a time, but it was completely stripped except for a single hospital bed in the middle of the floor. A battery of surgical lights suspended from the ceiling over Daddy's bed cast beams of pure white. Humming machines with blinking red and green lights and tubes sprouting from their bottoms and sides stood haphazardly about. I shivered in the cold. Armed Secret Service agents stood in the shadows.

THE BROKEN ROAD 185

Daddy opened his eyes and looked at us when he heard Cornelia's voice. "We are all here with you, George. You are going to get over this. I promised you we were going to take you home and we will," she said.

Daddy's right arm where he had been shot was bruised and swollen to twice its size. Bags of medicine hung on IV poles stationed on one side of the bed.

"Hey, Daddy. This is Peggy," I said. "I came to see you as fast as I could." I began to cry. Daddy looked my way. "Now, sweetie, don't you cry. It's going to be all right."

Later, they told me the person who shot Daddy was a man named Arthur Bremer.

The following day, Daddy was removed from the critical list. He had won the Michigan and Maryland Democratic primaries. We were told that he would be a paraplegic for the rest of his life.

Daddy remained hospitalized at Holy Cross Hospital for fifty-three days. Thousands of letters poured in to the hospital as well as the governor's office. Even with volunteers and additional staff, the volume was overwhelming. Over twenty thousand responses were sent on directly to his office for reply, thousands more diverted to two colleges for handling, while thousands more were never acknowledged at all.

Some of the letters suggested miracle cures, special diets, medical devices, and the laying on of hands to heal him from his paralysis. They were reminiscent of many of the letters that Mama received in the midst of her struggle with cancer. It was inspiring to know that so many people cared.

On July 7 a military hospital plane touched down at the Montgomery airport. A large crowd cheered and cried as they

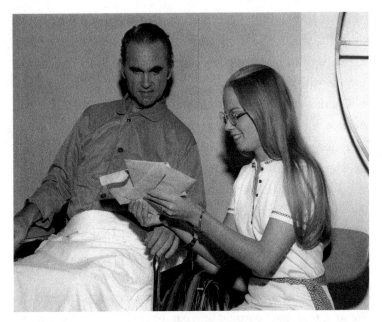

*Me and Daddy reading "get well" letters at Holy Cross Hospital in
Silver Spring, Maryland, 1972.*

saw Daddy in a wheelchair for the first time. Although his voice
was weak, the well-wishers buoyed his spirits. He had come to
reclaim the governor's office from the acting governor, Lt. Gov.
Jere Beasley, amid the rumors of a Beasley power grab that were
being fostered by Wallace insiders who were buried deep in the
piggy banks of state service contracts: food providers for state
cafeterias, road-building and printing contractors, administra-
tors of the state's health insurance and pension funds, state
boards, bridge construction and maintenance companies, university and community college services, and more.

The real motivation behind Beasley's ousting may have been
his penchant for honesty. Sighs of relief from the Wallace insiders

were heard all across the state when local television stations announced, "And now we are going live to Montgomery where an Air Force C-147 hospital plane carrying Governor George Wallace and his family has just landed." In less than an hour, the hospital plane took off heading south to Miami and the Democratic National Convention. Daddy was the governor of Alabama again.

Daddy spoke at the convention on the evening of July 11. His bodyguards lifted Daddy in his wheelchair to the stage. The Wallace delegates along with the majority of others stood and applauded. Although he was obviously in pain, his voice was strong as he spoke about returning to the values of the average working-class man and woman.

The following day, Daddy was nominated for president. He received 23.5 percent of the convention vote and earned 382 delegates, putting him third in the final count. Some said it was the height of his political career. As he was wheeled off the podium, no one could have imagined Daddy would run again for president in 1976 and serve two more terms as governor of Alabama; most people assumed George Wallace's political career was over.

THE DAY AFTER his appearance at the convention, Daddy was flown to the hospital in Birmingham for an emergency surgical procedure to treat internal infections caused by perforations of his intestines when he was shot.

After Daddy recovered from his surgeries, he was admitted to the Spain Rehabilitation Center at the University of Alabama in Birmingham. It was time for him to accept the new reality of the rest of his life as a paraplegic. His battle with depression and a growing dependency on pain medications soon overwhelmed him. While he was at Spain, he met a young woman who was a quadriplegic as a result of a motorcycle accident. The driver of the motorcycle, her fiancé, was not injured. He, along with her parents, had long since abandoned her. She was alone. Every day, Daddy visited her. Following her release, he called her often. Their friendship led him to speak frequently to others with paralysis and to promote funding for research.

IN LATE MAY, after the assassination attempt, I returned to Montgomery to try to salvage what I could of my spring quarter

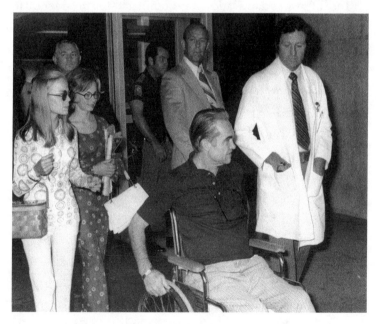

Daddy leaving Spain Rehab in Birmingham, Alabama,
August 1972.

classes at Troy. With an uncertain future ahead, it became obvious to me that a college degree was more important than ever. At least by the spring of 1973, I would have a teaching degree in hand. The prospect of being on my own became real; Mama and Mamaw were both gone. Mamaw had died of cancer on January 2, 1971. Mr. Henry, heartbroken yet again, moved to a small house in Tuscaloosa to live with his sister. There was no more broken road to go to.

BEFORE DADDY LEFT the rehabilitation center to return to Montgomery, the mansion went through a transformation. Its staircases, narrow halls, bathrooms with no showers, open second-floor galleries, and exterior steps to every entryway would make it difficult if not impossible for a paraplegic to live there. The upstairs sitting room and the connecting hallways on both sides that were open for view from the first-floor entryway were walled up. Bulletproof glass covered all the second-floor windows.

Halls and interior doors were widened. The master bedroom closet fell victim to a doorway cut into what had been my bedroom when we first moved to the mansion. It would serve as Daddy's therapy room. What had been my bathroom was gutted to install fixtures to accommodate the needs of who my daddy would be when he came home—a man paralyzed for the rest of his life.

An elevator, installed in a newly constructed tower in the rear wall of the mansion, was the only means to carry Daddy upstairs. Exterior ramps appeared at designated entryways, and the family dining room furniture was replaced. The mansion was ready for his return.

When Daddy came home, he felt the absence of the constant coming and goings of the therapists and doctors who had attended him at the hospitals. His physical and mental condition worsened. Although Daddy's doctors warned him of the dangers of drug dependency, his demands became more frequent and his personality more sinister.

We were soon living in the midst of what felt like a Southern gothic nightmare. Daddy's angry outbursts increased and were often directed at us. There was no give and take in his conversations with me, no interest in my life and what I was doing apart from him. He demanded sympathy.

For the first time in his life, Daddy had no choice but to live with us rather than around us. Throughout his life, Daddy's passion had been people, the kind that sat around the town square, gathered in small-town restaurants, or worked in the fields. His style of politics was all about racing to the next hand to greet, climbing up on the front porches of wood-framed houses, heel-and-toe walking along sidewalks, and last-minute jaunts up just one last staircase to shake a fella's hand. Daddy's perpetual motion defined him, energized him, fed his overwhelming need to be present in the moment. Everyday worries could not catch up as long as he was moving. The legs that carried him were akin to an artist's hands. Lose them and the magic was gone. He would have to learn another way.

AS DADDY STRUGGLED with the challenges of his paralysis, his physical pain, and the new realities of his future, his inattention to the politics of the governor's office gave rise to warring factions within his inner circle. People were afraid. The Wallace brand had been supporting their families for more than a decade, and the mere thought of its coming to an end was unspeakable. No one had ever thought about a contingency plan in the event there were no more Wallaces. While Mama's death may have caused a significant setback, an unexpected and abrupt George Wallace exit from Alabama politics would have backlogged bankruptcy courts for years. State employees would have jobs no matter the outcome of Daddy's medical challenges. But the two *c*'s of the Wallace brand, *contracts* and *campaigns*, were uncertain.

"The suggestions of the press that I am unable to fulfill my duties as governor are just another attempt to undermine the wishes of the people of Alabama," Daddy said as media outlets began to question his ability to serve out his term. Rumors of his depression and drug addiction spread. The *Montgomery Advertiser* called on Daddy to immediately retire. According to some members of the press, the governor's office was besieged by power brokers and Governor Wallace was in no shape, physically or mentally, to carry on. While many agreed, Wallace supporters rose up in righteous indignation and attacked both the article itself and its author.

The challenge to Daddy's authority was in some way more therapeutic than the hours of physical therapy he endured. Perhaps he remembered what his father said to him when, as a teenage boxer, Daddy would find himself lying on his back in the boxing ring: "Don't you just lay there, shake it off, get up and knock the little bastard's head off."

Daddy's ultimate recovery was a testament to his determination and courage. His coming to terms with his paralysis freed him from despair. But most important, his living with me rather than just around me changed my life. He was always there—he wasn't able to dash off.

AS WE ADJUSTED to our new reality, Cornelia took it upon herself to play matchmaker. In her view, now that I was at the age of twenty-two, it was time for me to get serious about finding a husband. Her list of eligible prospects was a veritable who's who of unmarried Alabama notables. When she found out that the Alabama Department of Tourism was planning an all-expenses-paid (minus spending money), ten-day excursion to Europe to promote Alabama tourism, she signed me up, perhaps hoping I would meet a prince. Daddy gave me a bon voyage hug and a hundred dollars. "Don't tell your daddy," Cornelia said as she slipped me a cash-filled envelope.

The mansion was decorated for Christmas when I returned. December 15 was the only occasion in my life when I had two dates on the same night. While Cornelia's quest for the perfect husband was ongoing, my first encounter of the evening was with someone I had never met and was arranged by my friend Benita, who had driven me from Troy to Montgomery on the day Daddy was wounded in Maryland, and her friend Carol Wells from Greenville.

"This is going to have to be no more than a meet and greet at your house," I complained over the phone. "I already have a date. The only reason I am doing this is for you. Now tell me his name again and where is he from?"

"His name is Mark Kennedy, and he's from Greenville."

"Never heard of him."

I walked up onto her front porch and rang the doorbell. I forced a smile as the door opened.

My future husband stood up and shook my hand.

During our brief conversation, there was no mention of politics or inquiries about my family. It was about me. There was no talk of connections, no "all of my family loves Governor Wallace" moments. I became uneasy. I had never lived outside the context of who my father and mother were and what they had done. Being in the center of a conversation was nothing new to me, but standing alone in the center of a conversation was.

After a pleasant but very ordinary chat, I offered my "Nice to meet you" and left. I gave Mark my phone number but was not sure he would call. "Nice enough, even looks a little bit like Daddy, meeting him made my friends happy, not a total waste of time," I said to myself.

"Sorry I'm late," I said as I sat down on the barstool next to my date for the evening. "I had to do a favor for a friend."

"No problem," he replied. "You want a Coke or something stronger?"

20

'Til Death Do Us Part

Southern mamas are known as being subtle, like a freight train.

—*Shellie Rushing Tomlinson*

When I met Mark in early December 1972, I hoped he was a person I could believe in, someone who was not likely to desert me, someone with roots in the ground who could perhaps help me grow my own roots. It was very important to me that I found him on my own. No matchmaking by Cornelia or the Wallace inner circle. Mark's distance from my family allowed me to make my own assessment of who he was.

The day after our "drive by to kick the tires" meeting, the intercom buzzer rang in the guesthouse. "Miss Wallace, there is a call for you from a Mark Kennedy. It came in on the public line, rather than on your personal line. Wanted to check before I put him through." The next day, a Sunday, Mark drove through the mansion gates in a 1968 maroon Tempest with a broken antenna and parked next to my new 1972 black-on-blue Mercury Cougar that Daddy had bought for me. Mark was on his way back to Auburn University some fifty-five miles away.

The following Wednesday I took Mark to the capitol to meet Daddy. His secretary cleared the room for us when we walked in. Mark and Daddy's conversation was casual. Daddy interrogated my new beau in a gentlemanly way. Mark had appropriate accolades for the Greenville, Alabama, Wallace loyalists, including the local probate judge and the owner of a local restaurant, which Mark professed was one of his all-time favorites.

As we exited, Mark no doubt heard the secretary's train-whistle whisper, "Is this the one?" At breakfast the next morning, Daddy looked over the top of his newspaper. "When are you two getting married?" he asked.

MARK MET CORNELIA, Ruby, and my extended family on Christmas Day. Cornelia imported a chef to assist the kitchen staff with the preparation of our "Christmas à l'Orange" extravaganza. Two large candelabra holding orange-scented candles sat amid orange blossom bouquets in the middle of the mansion dining room table.

We sipped fresh-squeezed orange juice in the First Lady's Room and then sat down to a dinner of duck à l'orange, creamed sweet potato orange cups, orange-glazed squash, orange bread pudding, and ambrosia. Daddy surveyed the Christmas feast.

"What is all of this?" he asked.

"It is our Christmas dinner, George," Cornelia shouted from the other end of the long table.

"I know that," Daddy grumbled. "But what is it?"

"We are having an orange-themed Christmas."

Daddy snorted. "Well, back in Clio, all we ever got for Christmas was an orange and maybe some candy, when I really wanted a bicycle." He reached beneath the table and pushed a buzzer that rang in the kitchen. The server appeared. "Go see if you can find me some barbecue," Daddy said.

Following Cornelia's flight from the table, the plates began to pass.

"I promise you, it is not always like this," I said to Mark.

"Want an orange roll?" he asked.

"Anybody got any vodka to put in this orange ambrosia?" Ruby said. "We could all stand a screwdriver after this mess."

THE MIAMI DOLPHINS and the Washington Redskins were playing Super Bowl VII on January 14. A perfect season was on the line for Miami. Mark and I watched the game in the guest-house. Miami won 14–7.

After it was over, we walked outside. Mark was working on a class assignment and wanted to get back to Auburn before the library closed. He gave me a modest hug.

"I wish you didn't have to go," I said in a damsel-in-distress voice.

Mark smiled, "And I wish I could stay here forever."

"You can!"

Mark looked at me, puzzled.

"You just asked me to marry you, right?" I said.

IN APRIL, MARK and I attended a benefit concert at Garrett Coliseum. A news photographer spotted an engagement ring on my finger and asked if he could take a photo. The following day, the picture of my engagement ring, along with my beaming face, was published on the AP wire service. The caption read something akin to "Peggy Wallace, the daughter of Alabama Governor George Wallace, shows off her engagement ring at a recent event in Montgomery, Alabama. Sources say she and her fiancé, Mark Kennedy, met on a blind date last December. No word from the governor's office yet."

In the aftermath of his assassination attempt, Daddy decided he was losing his grip on the loyalty of his supporters. At his direction, the governor's office mailed more than forty thousand letters to Alabama high school seniors as well as to every teacher in the state. Photos of him and Cornelia arrived in the mailboxes of every resident of every nursing home in the state. He ordered his signature placed on diplomas from all state colleges and universities. The phone lines in the governor's office were busy with staff and volunteers phoning to say, "Governor Wallace asked me to call to say hello and to see if there is anything he can do for you."

ON MAY 29, Buckingham Palace announced the engagement of Queen Elizabeth's daughter, Princess Anne. She was to marry on November 14, 1973.

"Well, hell, Cornelia," Ruby said upon hearing the news. "We'll just have a royal wedding of our own." Cornelia agreed. On August 5, the governor's office officially announced my engagement to Mark. We were to be married on December 15, 1973.

One of the mansion bedrooms was cleared and converted into a wedding war room. Folding tables were set up amid snaking telephone cables, extension cords, stacks of wedding invitation boxes, and other miscellaneous items one would typically encounter in an "Alabama royal wedding office," including thousands of three-by-five index cards bearing names and addresses as well as personal notations on who the people were.

In 1959, the Alabama legislature had dumped the existing state flower, the goldenrod, in favor of the camellia. Although camellia blooms were not harvested for sale at florist shops due to their short lifespan, they were found in front yards, graveyards, and public parks in small towns and cities throughout Alabama, and they were in bloom.

On Friday, December 7, Wallace county coordinators and garden club members under the command of local florists launched Operation Camellia. Thousands of the flowers were picked, stems wrapped in paper towels dipped in water, put on ice in coolers, and driven to a cold storage facility in Montgomery, where florists picked them up. Each bloom was placed in a tube of sugar water and ultimately became part of bridal bouquets and arrangements in the nave and altar of my church. They were also in elegant arrangements and lit by candlelight inside the mansion, on its grounds, and in a billowing pink-striped tent where an orchestra played. It seemed that every single camellia in the state had made its way to my wedding

On the day itself, the organist played the bridal march. The congregation stood as I entered the church. A momentary pall fell over the church as the wedding guests saw Daddy sitting

Me, Mark, and Daddy on my wedding day,
December 15, 1973.

alone in the front pew, unable to turn and watch as I walked down the aisle.

Many of the guests wiped tears from their eyes as the reality of his humanity overcame them. For at that moment, he was merely a proud father of the bride, waiting for her rather than walking with her on her wedding day.

Mark and I, along with Daddy, Cornelia, and Mark's parents remained in the mansion solarium for hours shaking hands and thanking the thousands of guests who attended the wedding reception.

"It's just like I told you," a guest remarked after taking a bite of wedding cake. "They are family to me."

Finally, things quieted down. Friends lingered, wandering the mansion's grounds and enjoying themselves.

"If all this won't elect George Wallace, then I don't know what will," I heard Ruby remark. As usual, she was drinking whiskey.

Hardy late-night well-wishers gathered with the Wallaces and the Kennedys under the mansion's front portico as Mark and I walked quickly through a hailstorm of rice launched from hundreds of handmade pink satin camellias. Our limousine moved slowly through a waving crowd as we passed through the mansion gate.

The aircraft hangar was dark but for the ground lights of a small private jet. As the aircraft taxied to the end of the runway, one of the pilots opened the cockpit door. "All buckled up?" he asked. "Looks like we are going to hit some rough weather for a while after takeoff, but after that, it will pretty much be clear sailing." As the jet climbed through thunderheads, I looked out of the window. It was snowing.

THE *NEW YORK TIMES*, reporting on my wedding, stated: "It was, as one observer of Southern society noted, 'probably the most lavish social affair in the Cradle of the Confederacy in its long and illustrious history of colorful social events' . . . But it was readily apparent that it was far more than a social event. In fact, quite a few of the 8,000 invited guests likened it to the recent marriage of Princess Anne, and if royalty were measured by political achievement the comparison would not [be] too farfetched."

After Mark and I returned from our honeymoon in Mexico City, Daddy called us over to the mansion. "Now sugah, make sure you write everybody a thank-you note, you hear?" Daddy said, referring to all the thousands of people who had given us a wedding gift. We spent the better part of the first six months of our married life writing to Dear So-and-So and thanking them for the lovely silver platters, china plates, assorted tablecloths, linen napkins, two vacuum cleaners, and a bronzed camellia, among many other gifts.

"We can pass these things down to our daughters one day," I said.

Years later, Mark would reply, "Do you really think our two sons will want all this stuff?

On June 4, 1974, less than six months after the wedding, Daddy received 65 percent of the votes cast in the Democratic primary and carried all of Alabama's sixty-seven counties in the process. (He had finally managed to change the succession law.) In the November general election, his vote percentage increased to 84 percent with 497,000 total votes cast for Wallace and 88,000 for his opponent. His 1974 wins, in both the primary and the general election, would be the largest margin of victory in his entire career.

On January 20, 1975, Mark and I attended the fourth inauguration of a Wallace on the steps of the capitol. It was sunny with a brisk north wind. With no parade or governor's ball to follow, the inauguration ceremony itself would take center stage. Daddy and Cornelia sat together at the front of the stage.

A woman sitting next to Ruby leaned toward her. "What is Cornelia wearing?" she asked.

"Well," Ruby replied, "that hat is called a tam, and that sash is held on with something called a kilt pin, and the pattern in that material is like a signal that a Wallace is coming."

"Well, it's very lovely and stylish," the woman replied.

Ruby turned and looked at her. "Honey, it's not about looking good. That getup means that the Wallace clan is back."

The woman paused. "Would that be with a *c* or a *k*?" she asked.

21

In Tents

*There are people who will stand up with you, but how
many will stand up for you?*

—*Peggy Wallace Kennedy*

When Mark promised to love me and cherish me " 'til death
do us part," I had no reason to doubt him, I just didn't
believe him. My lack of faith was not because of something
someone told me, it was the way I always had felt about Daddy.
I never knew which Daddy was on the other side of the knob
when I knocked on the door. Would he love me less or love me
more? "That's just the way he is," Mama would say.

That was *not* the way I wanted my life to be with Mark.
I wanted to stand on solid ground rather than on shifting sand.

My life had been a matter of surviving. I was usually focused
on the moment. There was no need to assume responsibility for
my own life. Decisions had always been made for me, which in
turn absolved me of the consequences of making bad decisions.

And then came Mark. If the marriage didn't work out, it would be my fault, which terrified me.

In Mark's family, his voice had always mattered, and he assumed it had been the same for me. When he refused to make decisions for me out of what he saw as my obligation to claim myself, it enraged me over what I saw as his desire to see me fail. He wanted me to be independent not only for myself but for him as well, so that he could breathe and have a life of his own. My desire to have Mark all to myself—after living a life of having no one just for me—suffocated him, and soon there was a wall between us. At the same time, it seemed that I could not live without him and he could not live with me. And we were both so young.

In August 1974, we moved to Birmingham. Mark went to law school and worked part-time in a congressional field office. I taught special education in the Birmingham school system. Very few people in our apartment complex knew who we were, but then neither did we! It was a difficult time for both of us.

Following Mark's law school graduation, we returned to Montgomery in the spring of 1977 and bought a small house not far from the Governor's Mansion. While Mark was looking for a job, I sanded and painted the floors, washed our clothes in the basement of the mansion, and tried to avoid Cornelia. By that time, her relationship with my father had devolved.

The very thing I had found so appealing when I first met Mark—his disconnection from the life of politics and power—proved to be a significant hurdle in the well-connected community of old-line law firms in Alabama's capitol. In 1977, a trial lawyer was a lawyer who tried cases in a courthouse; if there was a class action lawsuit it was either filed by the government or filed by someone who was suing the government, and most times the courthouse snack bar and grill was where cases got settled. For the most part, the practice of law in Montgomery was about civility and pedigree. Connections mattered, and having a Confederate general sitting on even a twig of a branch on the family tree was a mighty fine thing.

Mark was the son-in-law of a lame-duck governor who would be riding into the sunset in less than sixteen months, and the son of a church secretary and an insurance salesman from Greenville, Alabama. The cum laude ribbon attached to his law school diploma didn't get him past the law firm lobby.

To make matters worse, there was a tawdry scandal brewing in the Governor's Mansion that had become public. On September 7, the *Washington Post* published an article headlined MRS. WALLACE MOVES OUT OF THE MANSION: "A dark-haired mystery woman went around Montgomery at night, distributing photocopies of a divorce petition to newspapers, TV, and radio stations. One local TV reporter received a call from a woman who instructed him to go to a supermarket to the produce section and look beneath a pile of bell peppers. And there, among the peppers, was a petition for divorce."

The dark-haired woman was Cornelia, and the masthead of the petition read "In the Matter of Cornelia Wallace v. George Corley Wallace." It was going to be a bad run for the House of Wallace, and Montgomery law firms were taking sides.

In late September our phone rang. The call was for Mark. He was not at home. I took a message.

"You had a call from a Mary Owens," I said as Mark walked into the house. "John DeCarlo wants to meet with you. I have his number."

"Who is John DeCarlo?" We were both mystified.

It turned out that in February 1968, John DeCarlo, an attorney from Birmingham, had taken a leave of absence from the State Banking Department and joined Daddy's 1968 presidential campaign. It was he and two other Wallace appointees who were tasked with getting the American Independent Party on the ballot in all fifty states. Though naysayers had called it "Mission Impossible," DeCarlo and his team managed to organize thousands of volunteers who in turn collected 2,717,338 signatures. Later, during Daddy's 1972 presidential race, DeCarlo worked as an organizer and served as Daddy's attorney as well. On July 7, 1972, Daddy had appointed John DeCarlo to a seat on the Alabama Court of Criminal Appeals.

Mark returned DeCarlo's phone call the following morning. After a meeting several days later, Judge DeCarlo hired Mark as his staff attorney. DeCarlo and his secretary, Mary Owens, would play pivotal roles in Mark's career and in our lives.

IN LATE SUMMER of 1976, Daddy discovered that Cornelia, with the aid of a Folsom relative, had wiretapped his bedside telephone. Concealed wires were run through the bedroom wall and connected to a recording system hidden in the bottom cabinet of a floor-to-ceiling bookcase on the other side of their bedroom wall. The telephone by his bed had become his lifeline, for it replaced the roadways to the corners of the state and everything in between.

Daddy was famous for calling people all hours of the night. There were times when the answering party would hang up after commenting something akin to "Yeah, and I am Bear Bryant." His calls were about politics, business, encouragement for others, and most often for simple reassurances from friends and strangers who he had not been forgotten. But then there were the conversations with women, which in Cornelia's opinion were less than appropriate.

In Cornelia's mind, there were people who were plotting against her. She was the co-captain of the USS *Alabama Ship of State*, and more than just a few of the deck officers who needed to walk the plank. While her politically disconnected confidantes may have agreed with her view, the salty dogs of the USS *Wallace* did not. There would be no mutiny as long as they were sitting in the crow's nest.

After directing the mansion secretary, Millie Gallagher, and the rest of the staff to leave the premises and sending the mansion servants to their living quarters on the grounds, Daddy's personal security team began searching the second floor. After the recording device was removed, the search for the tapes themselves ultimately led them to a safe hidden away in the back of an upstairs closet. A stack of recordings was found inside. The tapes were removed, placed in a canvas bag, weighted down, and later that day thrown into the Alabama River.

A few days later, on September 8, 1976, Daddy held a news conference. "It was a purely domestic matter," he said. "There was no politics involved at all. No one has been hurt, no one has been harmed."

The following day, both he and Cornelia hosted a large reception for Rosalynn Carter at the mansion. It was a political event. Jimmy Carter was running for president at the time and Carter wanted Daddy's endorsement. Although there was little conversation between them, they were at least in the same room.

"I guess Cornelia's not going anywhere," one of the attendees remarked to a friend.

"Well," her friend replied, "if I did that to my husband, he would have thrown the cat and me out of the house. Let's go hug the governor's neck. He needs some tender loving care from somebody."

IT WAS DIFFICULT for me to understand how Daddy and Cornelia could get past what I saw as Cornelia's betrayal. For the most part, Mark and I stayed away.

"Let the smoke clear," Mark suggested.

"Why would Daddy want her to stay after all of this?"

"Maybe they didn't get all of the tapes." A year later, on September 6, 1977, the day after Labor Day, Mark and I drove through the mansion gates around three P.M. We were returning from a long weekend at the Beach Mansion. A small blue van was parked at the back door.

"There's Cornelia," Mark said as Cornelia walked past the van. "Do you want to say hello?"

"Of course," I replied.

Cornelia never looked our way as she continued toward a waiting car just in front of us.

"I guess she didn't see us," I remarked as she was driven away. "We'll catch her next time."

There was no next time. That was the last time I saw Cornelia. She moved out of the mansion and out of our lives. Cornelia and Daddy were divorced four months later, on January 4, 1978. Thirty-one years later, Cornelia died at the age of sixty-nine.

IN SPITE OF all the drama, Cornelia and Mark and I had been close. She was with Daddy during the darkest period of his life. But she never really did understand how the Wallace network operated.

As Daddy's wife and Alabama's First Lady, Cornelia thought she should come first, over all the others. In hindsight, perhaps I should have warned her, though I doubt she would have listened. There was too much to lose for the Wallace insiders if Cornelia had the power of the last word. Daddy didn't make the rules. He was too busy for that. He was the gate rather than the gatekeeper, and that made all the difference.

22

Testify, Brother Wallace!

In recognizing the humanity of our fellow beings, we pay ourselves the highest tribute.

—*Thurgood Marshall*

It was during this period that Daddy repented for his past actions with both words and deeds. He made outspoken declarations of his changed heart. His own suffering had contributed to the evolution of his thinking. He had come full circle, returning to the man he had been in Clayton as a young judge.

In 1979, at the Dexter Avenue Church where Dr. Martin Luther King had been the pastor and led the Montgomery bus boycott, Daddy made an unannounced Sunday visit. He was pushed up the aisle in his wheelchair to the front of the church. He spoke to the African American congregation: "I have learned what suffering means. I think I can understand something of the pain black people have come to endure. I know I contributed to that pain and I can only ask for forgiveness." And by and large, the African Americans in that church believed that he was sincere. They deeply believed in the power of forgiveness. It was one of the prime tenets of their faith. They respected his courage for coming into their midst and "testifying"—speaking from his heart and speaking the truth. When you testify, you say something important that comes from your heart and soul. And that's what Daddy did.

He would go on in the election to overwhelm his opponents in large part with African American support. It was African American voters who gave him one last chance to serve.

Some people may question whether Daddy's change of heart was sincere. I can say without a doubt that Daddy's testifying wasn't just talk. During his last term in office, beginning in January 1983, Daddy would appoint 160 African American Alabamians to state boards and agencies and double the number of black voter registrars in Alabama's sixty-seven counties. This was extraordinary, not just for Alabama but nationally. Daddy had done what he could to disenfranchise and even destroy the black community, and he believed that God struck him down for what he had done. He began to come to terms with the suffering he had caused others. There was a connection in his mind between his journey to redemption through suffering and African Americans' journey to freedom through suffering.

The author Stephan Lesher, in his 1994 book, *George Wallace: American Populist*, wrote about Daddy's changed heart as he came to "a humanity too often lacking in his actions; alone and crippled, forced to introspection for the first time in his life, he realized that though he had purported to be the champion of the poor and the helpless he had trampled on the poorest and most helpless of his constituents—the blacks."

I felt in him again the kind of father I once knew, the man who believed he could love us and still fulfill his lifelong dream of being governor of Alabama in 1958. The beauty and power of compassion had been revealed to him.

NINETEEN SEVENTY-NINE ALSO marked another important development in Daddy's life. In the late summer of that year, Daddy's limousine pulled into our driveway. One of his security men came to the door and rang the doorbell. There was a woman standing behind him.

"Who is that woman?" I whispered as the guard's companion, a platinum blonde woman in a very tight black sundress, followed my directions to the powder room.

"Well, let's just say she's your daddy's girlfriend," he replied. "I know, don't say it. But you have met her before. You just don't recognize her."

"How could I forget her?"

"Check out the lipstick when she comes back."

"Lisa Taylor!" I exclaimed when she reappeared. "So good to see you again. I loved that hot pink shade of lipstick you wore back in 1968, and here it comes again."

I chattered over my shoulder as I led the way. "Are the Mona Lisa Singers still on the road? Still playing the tambourine? Is Daddy coming in?"

However, the two questions that kept bouncing on the tip of my tongue but were afraid to jump were "What are you doing here?" and "Would you care for a modesty shawl to throw around that skintight sundress you have on?"

Lisa and Daddy had been close acquaintances for well over a decade. During the 1968 campaign, she and another female friend of Daddy's often played hopscotch up and down the aisle of his campaign plane, jumping from seat to seat toward the jackpot that was sitting in the front row with his feet propped up on the cabin wall.

Later, Lisa moved to Montgomery, taught school, and bided her time. Her love and long wait for Daddy paid off when, on September 9, 1981, Lisa and Daddy were married in the backseat of Daddy's Lincoln Town Car as it sat parked on the side of a country road in Autauga County, Alabama. Perhaps it was the limited seating that prevented me from being invited, much less having an opportunity to catch the wedding bouquet of, no doubt, pink roses.

Following the ceremony, Lisa was dropped off at the airport, boarded a private jet, and flew to Palm Beach, leaving behind a brief but touching press statement. "I just love the man." Following her foray to Palm Beach, the new Mrs. Wallace traveled to her hometown of Jasper, Alabama. It was more than a year before Lisa moved from Jasper to Montgomery. As Mamaw would have said, "She's a few bricks short of a full load." They may have visited each other and they probably talked on the phone, but it was bizarre—she just disappeared.

WHETHER DADDY'S LAST term in office was good for the state is up to history. And whether Daddy's marriage to Lisa Taylor was good for him was a subject for debate.

On January 18, 1983, Mark and I took our almost five-year-old son, Leigh, to his grandfather's last inauguration. We hoped that even at his young age, he would one day remember the occasion or find himself in photos taken that day. Mark was about to take a picture of Leigh and me standing in front of the bust of Mama that sat in the capitol rotunda. Before the flash went off, one of the capitol tour guides who had been greeting and giving tours since before Mama died walked up beside me. "Stay there," Mark said. "Let me get a picture of all three of you."

"Give me a hug," she said. "Your little one looks like his grand-daddy. Got that Wallace dimple going on."

"And he acts like him sometimes too," I said with a smile.

"Walk over here with me for a minute," she said. "Somewhere where nobody will be listening."

I handed Leigh off to Mark and followed.

"When I walked down there to the governor's platform to check on things," she said, "I noticed your name places were pasted on the chairs in the middle of the back row. Well, I knew that wasn't right, so I was pulling them off to move y'all up by your daddy when a man pranced up and asked me what I was doing."

"Who was he?" I asked.

"He said he was the new chief of protocol for the State of Alabama, whatever in the hell that is. Said his name was Jimmy Hatcher. Well, I happened to look down and damn if he didn't have on purple velvet shoes. Not really shoes, more like what ballet dancers wear. They had gold buckles. So I asked, 'Is that why you are wearing those purple velvet shoes?'"

"What did he say?"

She leaned in closer. "Get this. He says that the governor has a new family and I needed to leave those stickers alone. So you three get down there before the new family shows up, whoever in God's name they are, and grab you a seat."

As Mark, Leigh, and I walked down the capitol steps and onto the reviewing platform, the Wallace crowd waved and nodded our way. "At least those folks think we should be down here," Mark said as we ripped the stickers off three chairs on the second row.

The soon-to-be new First Lady was apoplectic when she saw us sitting there. No doubt the chief of protocol was going to receive a tongue-lashing before he could even take off his shoes.

THAT EVENING, AN inaugural concert was held in a local high school auditorium. A hand-held spotlight caught Daddy and Lisa coming down the center aisle. Although the First Lady's voluminous pink ball gown accented with pink hair ornaments may have seemed a bit overwhelming for a high school auditorium, it was no doubt lovely.

As the concert came to a close, family members, both new and old, were called to join Daddy and Lisa as the orchestra played "Stars Fell on Alabama." Leigh, dressed in a sailor suit, refused to take off his overly large Scooby-Doo sunglasses as he walked across the stage. With a need for a moment of hilarity in an otherwise ostentatious display, the crowd pointed to him and cheered.

Following the finale, Lisa was kind enough to walk over to me. "Well, your child certainly stole our show with those sunglasses on," she said.

"You're damn right he did," I replied.

As the three of us drove past the Governor's Mansion on our way home, Mark slowed the car down, as any tourist would have done, so that we could gaze through the mansion's wrought iron fence and into the golden glow of candles as the new Wallace family mingled about.

"Let's go home," Mark said. "I've had enough pink for a lifetime."

ON JANUARY 20, two days after Daddy's inauguration, the *Tuscaloosa News* published the reporter Jack Wheat's article titled "The Enigmatic First Lady." According to the interviewee, Louise Wilson, a close friend, almost like a mother to Lisa, stated that singing was only one of Lisa Taylor's interests. "She's a Bible scholar. She can quote Shakespeare with the greatest of ease. She plays the piano beautifully, she likes to read, she's interested in interior decoration, she's a horsewoman . . . She'll have interests. I think she has already shown that when she was campaigning and went to the steel mills."

As to the hat that Lisa wore to the inauguration, Louise said, "My telephone kept ringing off the hook the other day. People telling me how pretty she looked in that hat and they asked me if I had anything to do with it. And I said I wish I had."

According to the article, Mrs. Wilson was well known for making hats and in 1967 appeared on the television program *To*

Tell the Truth along with the hats she made out of Alabama forest products including wild hydrangea, pine cones, and mock orange.

Interestingly enough, just below the "Enigmatic First Lady" newspaper article there was a handsome photo of the "Little Mr. Snowflake Winners." According to *Urban Dictionary*, a "snowflake" is "a person who has an inflated sense of their own uniqueness and an unwarranted sense of entitlement."

"That little snowflake picture right underneath that Lisa article was an act of God," Mamaw would have said.

While Lisa was standing beside Daddy on his inaugural day, a friend of mine told me she heard the woman next to her lean over to her husband and say, "If Cornelia Wallace looked like she just stepped off a train in some village in Scotland, with that tam o'shanter hat she was wearing back during her days, Lisa Wallace looks like she just fell off a train in Russia with that beige seal fur skullcap she's got pasted on her head."

Several days later, Jimmy Hatcher, the new and only state chief of protocol in the history of Alabama, was no doubt wearing his velvet shoes when he called me at home and invited me to tea at the mansion the following day.

"Peggy," Mark's secretary, Jeanette, said when I called her the next morning to tell her that I was taking Mark with me to the mansion, "Judge Kennedy has sentencing this morning. I don't see how we can reschedule his entire docket."

"Well, I may be on his next criminal docket if he doesn't go with me," I replied.

"Hold on, let me go in the courtroom and see what is happening." After a few minutes, Jeanette returned to the phone.

"The jury box is full of felons from the county jail, the second and third rows of the courtroom are full of the felons that got out on bail, and the deputies, parole officers, and lawyers are hanging around the district attorney in the back. I can handle this until the judge gets back."

The first day Mark walked into the Montgomery county courthouse and stepped into the reception area of his courtroom and office, his soon-to-be assistant, Jeanette Harris, looked up from her desk, smiled, and asked, "Can I help you?"

Jeanette and Mark still laugh at the rest of the story. After Jeanette asked him if she could be of assistance, Mark told her he was the new judge. Then there was dead silence, until she said, "You have got to be kidding me." Mark was twenty-six.

On the day Mark retired from the Alabama Supreme Court, twenty-one years later, Jeanette was still by his side. "You've come a long way since that first day I met you," I heard her say. "Because I was smart enough to know you were smarter," Mark replied.

IN JANUARY 1983, if not before, Jimmy Hatcher was no doubt Alabama's most notorious thespian. And according to him, he was "thrilled to the moon and back to be appointed as Alabama's chief of protocol." I couldn't help but wonder whether Daddy's favorite dish, sardines and saltine crackers, would be served on the state china, garnished with watercress.

While there was neither a job description nor any historic precedent as to what an Alabama chief of protocol's duties would include, Chief Hatcher's first official act was to rename the state jet *The Lovely Lynda Lisa* in honor of the First Lady. This lovely new name was emblazoned in hot pink fluorescent paint on both sides of its fuselage. *The Lovely Lynda Lisa* would soon become the darling of control towers across the nation.

JIMMY HATCHER WAS born in Enterprise, Alabama, a midsized town in southeast Alabama. Like so many other towns that stretched along the soil of the Alabama Black Belt, it had risen to prosperity amid white blankets of cotton. That is, until the boll weevil showed up and laid waste to "the land of cotton." Then, thanks to George Washington Carver, a former slave who became world-renowned for his research on the many uses of peanuts, Enterprise was reborn as the peanut patch of south Alabama.

In the middle of the Enterprise downtown district, there is a monument in honor of the boll weevil. The oversized cast-iron insect sits atop the outstretched arms of a female figure dressed in cascading robes as she stands in a fountain of falling water. Talk about Southern! In December 1982, in Enterprise, the only two things that were made in France were the statue of a woman holding up a foraging insect pest and the purple velvet shoes that would carry Jimmy Hatcher to the Governor's Mansion the following month.

Mark's calendar was cleared so that he could go with me to the mansion. As we approached, the front door was flung open. "Welcome, welcome, on behalf of the governor and First Lady of Alabama, to the Alabama Governor's Mansion," Jimmy Hatcher said. "I am so honored to serve the First Family as the chief of protocol. This old house is about to become a haven of peace and tranquility for those that abide here."

Mark looked at me and gave me the smile that said "We can do this."

"The governor is in the private dining room having breakfast. He has requested that you have an audience with him before we have our chat," Hatcher said. "I assume you know the way."

"If this is not the most ridiculous thing I have ever seen, I don't know what is," I said. "Let's say hi to Daddy, see if any of my friends are still working in the kitchen, get the meeting over with, and go to lunch."

Mark and I walked into the dining room to see Daddy. A woman sitting in the chair next to him turned to me and said: "You are not allowed to be in here. This area is restricted."

Daddy stared and said nothing.

"That man looks like he's a prisoner in his own house," said Mark as we backed out the door.

"I WAS LED here by God," said Irene McDonald, the woman who only a short while before had thrown me out of the dining room. She settled into a chair across from us in the mansion sunroom. "I praise God's name for the life of your father and his First Lady. I prayed and God told me to come to this house. What I am to Lisa is a praying mother. I am her friend. I protect Lisa. I am someone Lisa can trust and talk to."

Irene's piety fit right in with the pink script on the fuselage and the purple velvet shoes—they were all part of a tableau of Southern absurdity.

Her matronly business attire, a modest wool nubbin dress and matching jacket, was accessorized by a pair of reading glasses hanging from a decorated cross clip; a ballpoint pen attached to a black string lay in her lap. *I would have liked to see you and my mother square off*, I thought to myself. *Lurleen Wallace would have decked you with just one punch.*

Mr. Hatcher joined us. "Please sit," he said, taking charge and pointing to a sofa on the sun porch.

"My dear Peggy," he said when we were all settled. "The governor wants this to be a home, something that he has never had. He wants to be happy for the first time in his life. I love our First Lady Lisa, and I am going to help her fill this house with happiness."

Irene interrupted. "I don't enjoy small talk when there is business at hand, so, Mr. Hatcher, if I may, let's just get to the point. Take a moment to read this." Irene handed us a document entitled "Admission to the Mansion and Grounds."

I read the document with growing alarm. My first reaction, rather than anger, was fear for Daddy's safety. As we were sitting there, all of the locks on the second floor were being changed to deadbolts.

"Now, we are going to go over every item with you so that there will be no misunderstanding," Irene said. "Rest assured, a breach of these rules will result in an immediate expulsion and potential arrest. There will be no exceptions. Now, as you will read, no one is allowed on the grounds without twenty-four-hour's notice. When you arrive at the gate, you must state your name, your purpose, and what area of the grounds or the house you intend to visit. Failure to follow this simple request will result in your expulsion. The troopers at the gate will call into the home and request permission for you to enter. If allowed, you will be escorted to a parking spot and accompanied by a law enforcement official at all times. No one will be allowed on the second floor at any time. If approved, your escort will show you to the area you have requested. There will be no wandering around."

"If Mama were alive, that woman would be staked out in an ant bed by now," I said as we drove off the mansion grounds.

Several weeks later, Mark and I took Leigh to the mansion to have his picture taken on the mansion's staircase in the entry hall. I had obtained prior approval as required. A state trooper followed me inside and stood to watch.

"While we are here and Leigh is dressed up, let's take a photo of Leigh in front your mother's portrait," Mark suggested. Mama's portrait, along with those of all of the other former First Ladies who previously lived in the mansion, hung in the sitting room adjacent to the foyer.

Mark pointed to the portrait in the next room. "That's your grandmother," he said to Leigh.

The trooper stood in the open entryway to the sitting room. "I can't allow you to go in there," he said. "You are only authorized to take photos on the staircase." With Leigh trailing behind, the three of us walked into the room. "After I take this picture, you can arrest all three of us if you want to. Now that would be a judge, a daughter of two governors, and the grandson of two governors," Mark replied.

Both Mark and I knew that all the mansion guards and the staff from the cooks to the gardeners were our friends. Many of them had been there when I was a child. They were in the same situation we were. As we were heading back to the car, we apologized to the trooper.

"It's really bad over here, isn't it?" Mark said.

The trooper didn't answer.

In the midst of this farce sat Daddy, wheelchair-bound and often in pain. He was serving what would be his last term in office.

WHEN I REFLECT on the years of Daddy's last term as governor, I think of Daddy in his wheelchair, vulnerable and out of touch. He was often isolated and alone. What could have been his last four years of opportunity to reclaim the love of his family, to tell stories to his grandsons as the grandfathers of their friends would do, was severely hampered not only by Daddy's health and lack of vitality but by his personal circumstances.

In early January 1983, prior to Daddy's inauguration, Lisa invited Mark and me to dinner at their house. After our meal, Daddy excused himself, as was his custom, and left the table. In the midst of a reasonably normal conversation, Lisa insisted that Mark persuade Daddy to have a new will prepared that made provisions for her.

"George is not going to be long for this world, and for me to stay I have to be provided for," she said. The conversation was more than strange to me. Daddy was about to be sworn in as governor for a four-year term.

"I wonder what she knows that you don't?" Mark asked as we drove home.

ON FEBRUARY 21, 1984, Daddy was admitted to a Montgomery hospital for what was diagnosed as a colon infection. Lisa called to tell me that Daddy wanted privacy. "There is not going to be any more traveling for him," she said.

Less than a month later, on March 11, Daddy was readmitted to the hospital for a reaction to medication. In both instances, following his discharge, his condition worsened. Daddy's long-time valet and caretaker, Eddie Holcey, who had looked after Daddy for years and was close to him, was now banned from the second-floor living quarters.

On March 19, Daddy's detail of security officers entered the Governor's Mansion without notice. After gaining access to the second floor, they took Daddy to a waiting ambulance parked at the rear of the mansion and took him to UAB Hospital in Birmingham. They remained with him and refused to allow any visitors without their permission. He was discharged a week later. "This is the second time we saved his life," one of the security officers told me.

On the afternoon of July fourth, after returning from an outing with Daddy, Lisa fired Eddie. Two days later, following Lisa's departure on a trip, Eddie was rehired. "I can do without y'all," Daddy said to Mark. "But I could never do without Eddie."

On September 1, 1984, Daddy was admitted to the hospital for still another reaction to medication. And on September 27, he was hospitalized for two weeks for a urinary tract infection.

On July 9, 1985, a fire heavily damaged Daddy's private resi-dence, which was vacant at the time. Although the point of origin was determined to be in the interior of the house, the cause was undetermined. Following the house's repair and renovations, Lisa left the mansion and moved to Daddy's newly refurbished house in January.

Daddy was notified several months later that a state audit of the mansion's furnishings revealed that seventy items, including historic furniture and art, were missing. The mansion property manager stated that most of the items had been moved to Daddy's house when the First Lady had taken up residence there. In November of that year, an audit indicated that while thirty items were returned, the rest could not be found. Daddy's office issued a terse statement to assure Alabamians that Governor Wallace had always been an honest man and would never have taken items that did not belong to him.

Although the charge was serious, Mark and I both had to laugh at the thought that Daddy would steal furniture. "He wouldn't even buy Mama a new sofa after his cigar caught the one we had on fire!" I told Mark.

ON MARCH 27, 1986, Mureal Crump, an officer at AmSouth Bank, where Daddy and Mama had banked for years, came to Mark's office at the county courthouse. According to Mr. Crump, the issue of Daddy's AmSouth Bank campaign accounts was the subject of a meeting he had with Daddy and Lisa at the mansion.

"I was caught in a crossfire between the governor and Mrs. Wallace about those accounts," he explained. "Lisa became angry and made threats of what she would do if George refused to transfer all the money in those accounts to her. Finally, the governor just gave in. I felt I needed to let someone know. I'm not sure George wanted to do that. There was over four hundred thousand dollars in those accounts." Following the meeting, Mark called Uncle Gerald. Within a week, what remained of the money was transferred back into the original accounts.

Lisa and Daddy were divorced on January 29, 1987, just weeks after his term as governor expired. In the span of less than two weeks, Daddy had retired from both politics and marriage. Daddy's last term as governor was no doubt the most challenging time in his life. He missed the opportunities to be with us. He was in and out of the hospital and always overmedicated. What should have been his personal victory lap was taken from him.

But there was still time. His determination to reclaim the high ground of asking for and receiving forgiveness kept him going. And that is the period of Daddy's life that I hope Leigh and Burns will think of first when they think of their grandfather's legacy.

"Daddy, we came to visit," I said as we walked into his bedroom soon after he left office and moved back to the house on Fitzgerald Drive. Eddie waved at us from across the room.

Daddy's room was very large, with a door opening onto a covered patio so he could sit outside. Most of the time, he lay in a hospital bed. He had a tray that he could roll up to the bed where he kept all his things—his billfold crammed with names and numbers but usually without cash, Garcia y Vega cigars, an always overflowing ashtray, and several lighters. After I visited with Daddy, I usually had to change clothes when I got home to rid myself of the smell of smoke. The curtains in the room were always drawn and the decor was bland.

The only personal picture on the wall next to Daddy's bed was a black-and-white eight-by-ten photo of him in a boxing match in 1933. His opponent, a student at Tulane University, is in a defensive stand, his head turned to the right, eyes closed, and blood below his nose and on his arm. Daddy is untouched. His right arm is extended into his opponent's chest.

Daddy spent most of his time paging through the morning and afternoon papers, sometimes talking on the phone, and seeing visitors from time to time. His forays of riding through the countryside, usually toward Clio and Clayton, became less frequent as time passed.

"GOVERNOR, PUT THAT cigar in your ashtray. You can't smoke and hold a baby at the same time," Eddie said. It was November 1988.

"Okay, sugah. Hand him over," Daddy said as he raised his arms.

I hoisted our son Burns onto his bed.

"He's got those bright eyes like Lurleen had. Can he talk?"

"Paw Paw, he's only three months old!" ten-year-old Leigh said as he climbed up on Daddy's motorized bicycle and turned the switch to high. The bike was supposed to help with Daddy's blood circulation in his legs, but that required Daddy to ride, which I am sure he never did.

"You need to take that thing home if Leigh wants it," Daddy said. "I don't know why they put the thing in here by my bed in the first place. Can I smoke a cigar while the baby's in the room? You know Eddie just had a baby. Was it a boy, Eddie? Sugah, hand me that channel-changer over there. Game's on. When's Christmas?"

"Daddy, we just got past Thanksgiving," I said.

"Well, buy these babies a Christmas present from me. I'll pay you back, just get me a copy of the bill. Don't go and spend too much now. Just a little something."

I looked across the room at Eddie and smiled. "Well, I guess it's all about family after all," I said.

Some months later, a state trooper assigned to Daddy called the house. He was new on the job. "Mrs. Kennedy, I hate to bother you," he said. "But there's a problem over here at the residence and I need some advice."

I handed the phone to Mark: "This is for you to deal with."

The trooper told Mark that Lisa Taylor Wallace and a young man had just pulled up in front of Daddy's house in a canary yellow Mark IV Lincoln Continental. When Lisa stepped from the car, the trooper recognized her from a photo in the security office with an attached note that she was not allowed on the premises. So he walked up to the gate and asked her and her friend, who had stepped out of the car at that point, to leave.

"I asked politely several times," he said. "But instead of leaving, she charged the gate and was attempting to climb over it. The young man was in the middle of the street screaming. I couldn't call for backup because my radio was in the guard shack."

"Well," said Mark, "you obviously did something, because you are on the phone with us."

"That's the problem," he replied. "I handcuffed her to the gate so I could call you."

"And, let me guess, all hell has broken loose."

"And then some," the trooper said.

23

Stepping Down

Each person must live their life as a model for others.

—*Rosa Parks*

D addy left the capitol grounds in January 1987 after serving four terms as governor. It was more than just the end of a political career. It was the end of a way of life for three generations of the Wallace extended family of friends, families, and supporters. The era of nighttime rallies in courthouse squares, of working in vacant storefronts scattered down the main streets of towns, of folding, stamping, mailing, and calling in three shifts a day and feeling moments of exhilaration when you shouted into the phone "Tell the governor we carried the county again" were gone. The shades were drawn on what many saw as the greatest moments of their lives. WE LUV OUR GOV bumper stickers were packed away for the last time.

ON JANUARY 19, 1987, I watched as Daddy's security team wheeled him off the inaugural platform as his successor, Governor Guy Hunt, succeeded him. Ten days after Daddy's last day as governor in 1987, he and Lisa were divorced. Perhaps power is a simile for love.

Following Hunt's inauguration, Mark, Leigh, and I visited Daddy at his house on Fitzgerald Drive. We sat by his bed, mostly silent, as the smoke from his red-tipped cigar began to fill the room.

"Sugah," he said, "go crack that side door."

Small talk seemed trite. What could we say? That he had had a great run? That now he could do whatever he wanted? Enjoy his free time? Go fishing? Daddy had no life aside from politics. So we sat, arms folded tight across our chests, directionless and numb with a sense of diminishment and loss.

Following several minutes of silence, Daddy refired his cigar, pushed himself up in his bed, and began to talk. We quickly had the sense that this was a historic moment, and Mark took extensive notes. Daddy covered many facets of his career. I think he was telling the truth as he knew and felt it. We were astonished: it was unlike him to reflect in this way.

ON SEGREGATION

I was never against the blacks. I never, in any of my speeches, made slanderous or derogatory comments about the blacks. Folks like Hugo Black, Ervin, Lyndon Johnson, Stennis, Faubus, all of them were staunch segregationists. While I was a moderate on those issues, those men had already preached separation of the races. Before 1957, Johnson was leader of the fight against the Civil Rights Bill in the Senate. One of Hugo Black's campaign posters back in the twenties read, "Keep Alabama White, Vote Black." I resent the continuing branding of me as a racist. All those folks have been rehabilitated. I outlasted them. Maybe one day I'll be rehabilitated too. The issue that I felt so strongly about was the issue of the growing federal bureaucracy and how it would devastate the state's sovereign power.

ON THE STAND IN THE SCHOOLHOUSE DOOR, JUNE 1963

We had privately conferred with the Justice Department and Civil Rights Commission and told them that the University of Alabama would be integrated on a time-table we had set for 1964. They said that would be unac-ceptable. That pushed the issue and we were backed into a corner. I was determined that we would not have the bloodshed that had occurred in Mississippi, Tennessee, and Arkansas. I knew it was coming but I felt that I had a duty to the people who elected me. It was a mistake but I went to Tuscaloosa. I took the National Guard because I did not want agitators from out of state to cause a problem. They arrested a band of thugs right outside of Tuscaloosa on Highway 11 that were coming in from out of state and jailed them until the following week. There was not a bit of bloodshed in Tuscaloosa.

I staged four plainclothesmen outside that young girl's [Vivian Malone] door for a week. I told [them] that they were to arrest anybody who went by that dorm and yelled obscenities or the like. After a few days they called and reported that all was quiet and wanted to come back to Montgomery. I let them. I went on statewide television the next week and told the people of the state that anyone who committed an act of violence or broke the law was not doing anything but hurting the people of our state.

SELMA TO MONTGOMERY, MARCH 1965

Col. Lingo was a crazy and Bull Connor, he was a troublemaker who defied my orders. I had told him to stay out of Selma. Those folks had the right to march and I wanted them to do it. Lingo went over there and all hell broke loose. It was a terrible mess.

Several days after the march I received several of the organizers in my office, including Rev. Lowery. Before they left they all wanted and got an autographed picture of me, and one even leaned over me and whispered that he supported me and what I was doing for states' rights.

DR. MARTIN LUTHER KING JR.

People say that I was an opportunist. Martin Luther King was as much of an opportunist as any man that I have seen. He became wealthy promoting his cause. He was young and inexperienced but smart enough to seize the opportunity to make a name for himself.

J. Edgar Hoover called me in 1964 and began discussing King. He told me that King would not buck his department and that he could be handled.

They say no one knows who you really are, deep down and all tucked away, hidden by obligations to those you want to please or wanting something they have that you don't. It just might be better that way.

"George Wallace may have been a lot of things, but he was not insecure," a friend of mine once said. "He's got more gall in his little finger than most folks have in their whole body."

"You're right," I replied. "That is, as long as you just look at the wrapper and not take a peek inside." Daddy's insecurity was the engine that added horsepower to his already forceful mind.

Most of my life with Daddy was spent looking at the wrapper. Seeing what others saw. His casual clothes were his work clothes, he ate and ran from our kitchen table leaving us behind, just like he did in cafés, unless strangers wanted to shake his hand and talk. He slept because he had to.

What was he running from? Being alone? When asked why he always needed to be surrounded by people, he'd say: "Might want something; might need to tell somebody something; might need a witness to say I didn't say what someone else said I said. Besides, the more talking going on, the less likely we might say something worthwhile!" And he'd smile his tight smile, chomp down on his cigar, and pull on it, making its tip glow red.

I often asked myself what I was supposed to believe about everything that had been written and said about my father. I asked myself what obligations I owed to his memory. For me, there is no obligation other than the truth. My secret most important question was: Would Daddy be proud of who I am?

24

Benched

When I discover who I am, I'll be free.

—*Ralph Ellison*

During the late fall of 1987, I was content. At the age of thirty-five, Mark, whom Daddy had appointed as a circuit court judge in Montgomery County, was already halfway to retirement with no real worries about the future elections he would have to win. And Daddy's lifetime of politics was in the past.

The house we had always talked about building was soon to be finished. Leigh was nine years old. I could finally breathe. No more looking over my shoulder. The best days of my life were in front of me. Even the voice of "This is too good be true" had fallen silent.

That November, Mark decided to run for the supreme court of Alabama. Supreme court races in the past had been gentlemanly and restrained, with most advice on who to vote for coming from practicing lawyers. But the times were changing as big business and trial lawyers squared off against one another in a philosophical and financial battle relating to large civil judgments being handed down in courtrooms and most often upheld in the appellate courts. It was the era of tort reform. With significant stakes on the table, judicial races were about to change: high profile, big money, and perhaps a launching pad to the U.S. Senate or maybe the governor's office.

On my thirty-eighth birthday, January 24, 1988, Mark and I stopped by Daddy's house before meeting friends for dinner.

"You need to remind him today is your birthday," Mark said as we walked through the kitchen door.

"Guess I should have bought a card for him to sign for the scrapbook," I replied.

"Daddy, today is my birthday," I said as we walked into his bedroom.

"That's mighty fine, sugah," he replied.

Daddy turned his attention to Mark. "Now about this supreme court race. I gave you a good job," he said, referring to Mark's appointment to the circuit court. "And you are going to stay there. You are not going to run for anything else. Put that out of your mind."

"Well, Governor," Mark replied. "I appreciate what you've done for us. But I think I can win, and if I'm elected, I think I can do a lot of good in the state."

Daddy pointed his finger at Mark. "Folks are saying that all you have to do is get in with the Wallace crowd around the state, and you won't have to do a thing. But there is a lot of difference between you and me and your last name is Kennedy, not Wallace."

"Daddy, who told you that?" I asked.

"Doesn't matter who told me anything. You two do as I say." And with that, he turned his attention back to the television. "Turn that volume up for me." In Daddy's mind the conversation was over.

I walked to the head of the bed. "You are going to listen to me," I said. "I have been a Wallace longer than I have been a Kennedy, and I have enough of Mama in me to tell you that Mark is going to run for whatever he wants to and you can't stop him. And if you try, I have enough of you in me to make your life miserable."

Daddy looked at me. "Isn't today your birthday?"

"Don't you change the subject," I replied. "You never knew when my birthday was before now."

"Well, dahlin'," Daddy said, "sometimes you have to say things because that's what other folks want you to say. So now I can tell them I said it."

As we were about to leave, Daddy said, "You do have a lot of your mama in you."

IN MARCH 1988, when letters from Daddy wound up in Wallace folks' mailboxes asking them to support Mark in his race for the supreme court, it wasn't much, but at least it was reason enough to catch up with the old crowd.

In June, Mark won the Democratic primary, and in November he was elected to the Alabama Supreme Court. At the age of thirty-six, he became the youngest supreme court justice to be elected in Alabama history. And in between, on August 21, our son Burns was born.

*"My dad does Justice." —Leigh Kennedy. Justice H. Mark Kennedy
on the Alabama Supreme Court (back row on the right),
January 1989.*

"You timed that just right," Mark's mother said.

"Well, that's the least a politician's wife should do!"

MARK'S 1994 REELECTION campaign will always be remembered as one of the dirtiest judicial campaigns in American
history. Although he won, he would never be the same. His belief
in the dignity of public service as a judge was gone. The politics
of the election of members of the judiciary belied the character
of what a judge should be, much less uphold.

Mark's republican opponent, Harold See, was a graduate of the University of Iowa College of Law and a professor at the University of Alabama Law School. His name recognition among average voters was, for the most part, zero. "Never heard of the man," most said.

But Professor See's campaign advisor was Karl Rove, who first had to crush the reputation of Texas governor Ann Richards, with a whisper campaign claiming that she was a lesbian, so that his client George W. Bush could win the Texas governor's race and secondly crush Mark's reputation, with a whisper campaign alleging that he was a pedophile, so that his client Harold See could win Mark's seat on the Alabama Supreme Court. Karl Rove won one race and lost the other. And Rove's "scorched-earth" style of politics would later be called "Make America Great Again."

In 1983, the Alabama legislature passed the Alabama Child Abuse and Neglect Prevention Act. The act established a new state agency, the Alabama Children's Trust Fund, to address "the state's growing problem of child neglect and treatment." Mark was appointed as chairman of the board.

Most of Mark's spare time was dedicated traveling the state to encourage nonprofit organizations serving women and children at risk for violence to embrace the philosophy of prevention rather than treatment after an incident occurred. He spoke what he preached when he was a juvenile court judge: "All of our resources are spent after the fact, when the abuse and neglect of children has already occurred. We need to be focused on programs that provide services, protection and hope for at-risk families who can be saved before the damage is done."

Mark's campaign material in his second race for the Supreme Court displayed photos of him with children, as a reminder of his work as chairman of the Children's Trust Fund. But Karl Rove saw the photos in a different vein.

"This is an opportunity to create a whisper campaign. We can use law school students to spread the word back home that Mark Kennedy is a pedophile. No news reports, no ads. Just family talk mixed in with "How are you doing in law school?" Rove probably said. Because that is the way it happened. And it was all a lie.

Two years later, Harold See won his second race for the Supreme Court against a different incumbent and won. Every week, the justices gathered in the Supreme Court conference room to discuss pending cases. Harold See sat across the table from Mark.

Several months after See took office, he spoke to Mark in regard to the smear campaign he ran against him. When Mark came home that evening he told me Harold See said he had been totally unaware of " 'that whisper campaign,' as he called it. 'I would never have condoned such a thing.' "

"Was that all that he said?" I asked.

"That was about it," Mark replied.

"So, he never apologized? Is that right?"

Mark nodded his head. "That was all he said."

I thought to myself, Harold See did what Daddy did on the day state troopers attacked John Lewis on Bloody Sunday in March of 1965. "I never told Al Lingo to attack those marchers on that bridge." It was not Daddy's fault.

Hard to take, to say the least. You would have thought I had been put through the wringer enough times with my father's political life. Now here it was, perhaps even closer to home—the same opportunism and gutter politics. But one thing was different: Mark always put me and our sons first. He was always, always there for us. And that made all the difference.

On June 11, 1999, after serving twenty-one years on the bench, Mark retired. He was doing something for me, Leigh, and Burns that Daddy never did—he was coming home to us.

25

The End of an Era

Maybe all one can do is to hope to end up with the right regrets.

—*Arthur Miller*

On Sunday, September 13, 1998, we stopped by Jackson Hospital on our way home from church. After twenty-six years of paralysis and fighting back, Daddy was seriously ill with sepsis, a virulent bacterial infection.

"Daddy, are you sure you are going to be okay?" He nodded yes. We promised to return the following day.

That night, Mark and I were watching Gary Sinise accept an Emmy award for best actor for his portrayal of Daddy in the made-for-TV movie *George Wallace.* As Sinise began speaking, our phone rang.

It was my brother, George. "Peggy, you need to get back to the hospital."

By the time we got there, Daddy was gone.

TWO DAYS LATER, Daddy's body was returned to the capitol rotunda and placed on a bier in front of a marble bust of Mama where her body lay three decades before. Over the course of the day and night that followed, an estimated twenty-five thousand people—as many African Americans as whites—came to pay their respects.

Daddy had repeatedly called Mark and me to come visit him during the last two years of his life. These were often late-night visits. We'd come in and he would begin talking: "You know, I was wrong about race and segregation. I know that now. I've had a lot of time to think about it." It was clear that he was sincere and that he was ashamed and regretful. He would talk for hours, circling around these points.

I might have wanted a more personal apology and a recognition on his part of how his behavior had shaped my life in ways that had been damaging and difficult. But that wasn't who Daddy

Governor George Corley Wallace at St. Jude Catholic Hospital on the twenty-fifth anniversary of the March from Selma to Montgomery, March 1990.

was. I came to see that the fact that he brought us close to him again and again, time after time, and unburdened himself was his way of apologizing to me. It was what he was capable of, and I came to be satisfied with that—he *was* asking for my forgiveness, not only for the ways he had impacted my life but for the man he had been. And I did forgive him. And I loved him.

MARK AND I returned to the capitol just after midnight. We walked up the steps, passing the place where Daddy and Mama once stood before cheering crowds of thousands. A capitol guard asked the line of mourners to give us a moment. I pulled a small bag of M&M's from my jacket and put them in Daddy's right-hand coat pocket.

"Always the right pocket," he would tell me back in Clayton. "Sugah, if you've been good, look in my right-hand coat pocket. There will always be something there for you."

"IF IT WAS ninety-six degrees at your daddy's funeral, it must be at least a hundred and ten today," Mark commented. We were walking across the large blacktop parking lot in front of Walmart.

"There must be a hundred black cars in this parking lot," I said. We wandered around, refusing to admit to each other that we had forgotten where we parked.

"That may be true. But we may have the only black Volvo with a Clinton sticker on the bumper."

"You have a point."

An SUV pulled in a parking space just ahead of us. The driver got out and headed our way. We smiled as she walked up in front of us, hoping to avoid the worst nightmare of a family in politics. "You don't know me, do you?" "Of course we do." "Then who am I?" Instead, she said it for us: "You don't know me, but I work up at the funeral home where your daddy was brought. Peggy, I'm from Barbour County—just like you. We have always loved your family. Your mama was a special lady. She and my folks used to have coffee sometimes, right there across from the county court-house at Seale's Café. Those were precious times."

It was so blazingly hot and humid on the blacktop in the Alabama sun that all I wanted to do was escape and find our car. But I smiled—the practiced smile of the wife and daughter of elected officials.

"Clayton was a great place to grow up, and Seale's Café was the best," I said.

"Well, I don't want to keep you-all in this heat," said our new friend from Clayton. "But I was blessed, and I mean blessed to be working at the funeral home when your daddy was brought in. I could not believe my eyes, and I called Mama and told her that the governor had just come in. She was as excited as I was."

"I'm so glad you got to see him."

Mark's eyes cut toward me.

"What else was I supposed to say?" I channeled back via a slight shrug. The sweat stood out on my forehead and was rolling down my back.

"I was hoping that they would let me do something, but I wasn't sure," she continued without missing a beat. "Then, praise the Lord, the funeral home director came up to me and told me they wanted me to do his hair. I called Mama and told her, 'Mama, they want me to do the governor's hair.' She gasped into the phone, just *gasped*. So, I asked Mama, 'Mama, what am I supposed to say to him?' And she says, 'Honey, just talk to him. Just talk to him. Because he's home folks from Barbour County. He's just like us. You don't need to put on no airs for George Wallace!' So I did just that. I talked and combed and combed and talked."

By that time I was melting. We hugged each other, and I thanked her for taking the time to tell me about her encounter with Daddy.

After about five yards' worth of walking she turned back to me. "I forgot the most important thing of all. How did you like his hair?"

Perhaps it was a combination of the heat and my Barbour County manners that creased my mouth with a big smile—my best smile. "Honey," I said, "I have never, and I mean *never* seen that hair looking any better than it looked that day."

"Praise the Lord," she said. "You've made my day."

The inside of the Volvo was hot to the touch, but not as hot as the softening pavement. "Let the windows down," I said.

Hot air rushed around us. Mark turned to me and said, "You know, your daddy would have loved every word of that."

"He probably heard every word," I replied. "I loved that man."

Burns met us in the driveway when we drove up. "Leigh and I filled up the pool with new water. Come swimming with us, Mom."

I smiled. "That sounds like a good idea to me."

———

WHEN THEY WERE young, my sons would sometimes pull books from the shelves of our family history, with questions for me to follow. But none of what they read could adequately address or capture the essence of humanity that lay hidden beneath the overwhelming facts of what their grandparents stood for and what they did.

"Tell us more, Mom. What did you do back down there in Clayton when you were a little girl? What was Mawmaw Lurleen really like? Do you think she would come over to our house and sit outside with us and tell us stories? I bet Paw Paw, back when he could walk, would be up and down all the time. Would you let him smoke his cigar inside the house? Why did he do those things to other people?"

The spring after Daddy died was when Mark and I took Burns to Atlanta to visit the Martin Luther King Jr. National Historic Site and Museum. I saw Daddy through Burns's child eyes. I thought about who Daddy was when I was nine years old, living down in Clayton before he vowed never again to be "out-niggered," before he won the governorship, before the civil rights clashes of the 1960s and the era's fraught politics and tumultuous social change. I thought of Mama, Daddy, and me standing in the shade of an oak in the yard of my childhood when there was no burden to bear, no heartaches, and nothing to defend or explain away, when my parents were just like the other parents of Clayton, who sat on front porch swings while their children played in the yard.

26

Doors

*Although the world is full of suffering, it is full of the
overcoming of it.*

—*Helen Keller*

One day, a psychiatrist told me to draw a picture of myself. "That is me," I said, pointing at a stick figure with flowing lines of charcoal hair.

"What does the picture mean?" he asked.

I traced my finger along the drawing. "You see, I walked down the street to my house. I went inside, locked the door behind me, and turned off the lights."

Some days you wake up feeling fine and then depression taps you on the shoulder. "I'm still here," it says. "Always waiting for the next shoe to fall. And remember—it's better to be bitter than to feel nothing at all."

I would come to realize that depression had been with me for as long as I could remember. "Why, she's just a sad little thing," I heard people say about me when I was young. Then it became "What's wrong with her?" when I was grown.

Depression hides in the crack and crannies of life, oozing out like black tar. It's sticky and leaves ugly smears on whatever it touches. It lies low, like morning fog. It brings darkness and offers escape in days of dreamless sleep. It is a disease, not just a state of mind. Depression is not something you get over; it is something you climb out of. It's patient. It lies in wait inside you until a word, a song, a memory, or loss unlocks its cage. It encourages our mothers, fathers, husbands, and wives to ask "What's your problem?" or "You better be thankful for what you've got." And finally, "All I have to say is get yourself together. Get over this."

Depression taps at your window and scurries along the ceiling overhead at night while your family tries to make the best of it. "Let her sleep," they say. Not for your sake but for their own.

"Who wouldn't want to trade places with me?" I asked myself as I looked at blooming camellias through a wall of windows in my kitchen. I was the daughter of governors, I'd grown up living in a mansion with servants, had a husband at the pinnacle of what young lawyers dream of becoming and two beautiful sons.

The house I lived in was unique and wonderful, according to a reporter. "Why, it's akin to a little gem box," she said. The lines, angles, and artful views from nooks and crannies unsettled me. Bright spotlights on paintings, overly green plants basking in washes of morning sunlight, a lamp dimmed and glowing atop a perfectly situated end table that had once belonged to my mama—all this hurt my eyes and angered me. The perfection of my house—its shininess, bleached white walls, soothing grays— made me feel slipshod.

I hid my thoughts. Friends swooned as I gave them the tour. Unlike my house, which sang in perfect pitch, the choir in my head sang one of Daddy's favorite tunes, "You could be pretty if you wanted to." He said that to me one time; it has always stayed with me.

I would ask Mark: "Why does he say things like that?"

Is there nowhere in this place for me just to throw stuff on the floor? I sometimes wondered.

My depression would jump from behind a door or settle in the bed next to me. There had always been a fix, a string of psychiatrists and therapists, talking it out, sitting in the sun, a parade of colorful pills. Most days, I sat for hours, staring out a window, happy to wait until it was time for bed. I was no match for its ferocity. A cliff lay straight ahead and there was nothing I could do but close my eyes.

Mark tells me how beautiful the fall of 1995 was, how Leigh, as a high school senior, played with great heroics on the football field and how happy he was when he was named the most valuable player of the year and we all stood up and cheered at the football banquet when he was given his award. He laughs with our son Burns as they reminisce about Burns riding his "trick" bicycle in front of our house, then kicking up red dust as he made the perfect slide.

Mark smiles at me and I smile back, knowing that I have no memory of those moments in our sons' lives.

It was the Sunday after Thanksgiving. We were returning home from a long weekend visit with Mark's family. Burns and Leigh were in the backseat. I slumped in the passenger seat, fighting off the nausea that ran along beside the blinding pain of the migraine headache. I'd had them before and so had Mama.

It was after dark when we pulled into our driveway. We let our sons out of the car and went to the emergency room. "My wife has a migraine headache. She has them all the time. A shot and fluids will make her feel better," Mark told the staff.

The doctor was cautious. "I want to take some X-rays of your head to be sure everything is okay up there. Then we'll give you a narcotic to ease the pain."

When I returned from the scans, Mark and two doctors were standing in my room. A nurse came in and gave me a shot. I could tell by Mark's darting eyes that something was wrong.

"The X-rays show that you have some sort of mass behind your right eye," one of the doctors said. "We don't think it's anything to worry about, but we want to keep you overnight and do more tests in the morning."

The shot eased the pain in my head and lured me to sleep. Mark told me not to worry, and the door shut behind him. I glanced at the wall clock. It was a few minutes after ten P.M. I closed my eyes.

MARK WAS CALLED back to the hospital at one thirty A.M. The staff had found me in the stairwell, two flights down from my room, and managed, with some difficulty, to get me back into bed. I was emotionally unstable and combative and in restraints.

Mark was visibly shaken when he walked into the hospital room. I fought the restraints. "Why are you letting these people tie me up like this?" I shrieked. "Take me home right now."

A nurse followed Mark to my bedside. "The doctor instructed us to wait until you arrived to give her another dose of a sedative to calm her down. He thought it would be better for her to see a familiar face."

But Mark's presence had had the opposite effect. There he stood all perfect. His whole family would be like a gaggle of geese, wandering up and down the hall, taking over the waiting room, wringing their hands at the thought of how many problems that Wallace wife of his was causing him.

I could feel myself falling, being chased by demons. There was a gunmetal taste in my mouth. I heard a chair scrape across the floor and saw Mark walking around to the side of the bed. I told him that I needed to go to the bathroom. He helped me use a bedpan. I told him I was thirsty. He held a cup of water close, so that I could sip from a straw. Panic set in as I realized that he was not going to set me free.

IN THE MORNING, a cheerful nurse came in, sat on the bed beside me, and took my hand. She would eventually free me from the restraints and help me get changed into the clothes Mark brought from home, but only after she had regaled me with an embellished account of the day she'd met my daddy.

I was angry and threatening when the doctors arrived: an internist and a psychiatrist and neurologist. I insisted that I be allowed to sit in a chair. Before I was through with them, I would have their medical licenses. They told me the mass behind my eye had been determined to be of no significance and believed what had happened the night before was symptomatic of a "reactive psychosis caused by stress." They were confident that it would pass in a few days.

But it didn't.

"I'm not drinking anything until you tell me where I am."

"You're dehydrated, and if we don't do something about it they'll hook you up to an IV."

It turned out that I was in Birmingham at University Hospital. "You weren't getting better at the hospital in Montgomery so we brought you up here yesterday," Mark said. I had no memory of the move.

Several days later I had still not improved. It seemed my only option was a series of electroconvulsive treatments (ECT). They were going to be done in the basement of the Lurleen Wallace Tower that was ajoined to the hospital.

I USED TO wonder if the picture taken of my mama in the first few days of her governorship was meant to be her official photo. She is standing behind the governor's desk with her arms awkwardly splayed as if she had to hold on to something. Her red dress is cinched with a wide cloth belt of the same color. Telephone, dictation machine, and intercom cables on the credenza behind her. An arrangement of pink and purple flowers in an awkward vase. A too-heavy enameled pin on her dress collar. A lovely smile.

The Red Dress photo, as it came to be known, looks unstudied and casual. It was hung in public buildings, college auditoriums, and the hallways of state-run hospitals, including the hospital I was in. Improving mental health care in Alabama was one of Mama's signature accomplishments as governor. If Mama could see me now, I thought more than once when I was in the hospital, what would she say to me?

"Ready to roll," one of the ECT treatment nurses said each morning. "How many we got today?"

I was wheeled through the crowded hallways. Between the two elevators, one of which would take me to the basement to receive my treatments, Mama's Red Dress photo hung on the wall.

DADDY KNEW ALL about my health problems. He worried over them, and often became emotional when he spoke to me. He'd ask me if I was okay. He wanted me to promise him that I would get well. He never asked where I thought my depression came from, if there could be a connection between him and me.

After a week of treatments, Mark took me home. Leigh and Burns were waving at the end of our driveway. A WELCOME HOME MOM sign was stuck to the door. Life settled back into more or less predictable rhythms.

Happiness comes and goes. Contentment is often episodic. But chronic depression stays with you for life. Keeping it at bay is a challenge, but it is not an impossible task. Overcoming the shame of not being strong enough, of being unable to just suck it up and keep going, is the first step to hope, not for a cure but for an opportunity to live with depression and still feel well and find happiness in the smallest of things.

Several years after I was discharged from University Hospital, I went to the Lurleen Wallace Tower again, as part of an invited tour. The Red Dress portrait in the basement was gone. They didn't do ECT treatments there anymore. Instead, they used the facility for cancer research. It contained a large cyclotron. I was there with Burns and Mark, and it felt as though we were

"In the darkness there is light." —Peggy Wallace Kennedy.
Me and Mark, August 20, 1988.

supposed to be there together. When the tour was nearly finished, our guide told us there was one more thing we should see. In the main atrium, an entryway of glass and natural light, hung a new portrait of Mama. As Burns and I stood looking at her, a new certainty bloomed in me, the knowledge that she would have been proud of me for fighting through my depression. It was one of those stunning moments that take your breath away.

27

Letters from Baghdad

Wars are poor chisels for carving out peaceful tomorrows.

—*Martin Luther King Jr.*

I t was after midnight when we drove through the gates of Pope Air Force Base, on the outskirts of Fayetteville, North Carolina. After fifteen months, our son Army Captain Leigh Kennedy was coming home from the Iraq War.

Mark, Burns, and I joined a collective crowd of expectant loved ones in a large, unheated aircraft hangar. Some sat on wooden bleachers scattered about a concrete floor while others moved about to keep warm. A young woman, probably in her twenties, sat away from the rest of us. Her strapless evening gown was not made for cold nights in hangars. Next to her on the bench sat a pair of glittering high heels.

The crowd was diverse: a melting pot of race and religion. Our political views probably ran the spectrum. We were probably also divided in our opinion about the justness of the war that our soldiers were fighting. But in that moment our diversity was unimportant—we were all Americans.

The engines screamed as the DC10 raced down the runway. Then it slowed and turned, bringing our children, husbands, and wives back into our arms.

Behind a flag-carrying entourage of army officers and a military band, a young soldier was pushed toward the plane in a wheelchair. Injured in combat and sent home for treatment, he now wore a neck brace, and one of his legs was in a cast. A truck trundled out a large metal staircase. Two men descended from the plane, carried the wounded soldier up the steps and into the plane while the band played the "Army Song."

The night my son Leigh Kennedy arrived home from war,
March 19, 2008, at two fifty-five A.M.

The wounded soldier appeared in the plane's doorway, on his feet, supported on either side by two soldiers with whom he had served. The three linked arms and descended the stairs. They had gone to war together, and now they were coming home together. A cheer went up.

"There's Leigh. He just came off the plane," Burns cried. "Hey Leigh. Over here!"

Leigh embraced me. "Mom. I'm home."

IN JANUARY 2007, after Leigh deployed to the war in Iraq, the yellow ribbons well-intentioned friends tied around two of the front yard trees that Leigh climbed when he was a child only reminded us that he was gone. My pride in his call to serve did little to quell the fear that I would lose him, which haunted my days.

The American people were told the war in Iraq was fought to make America safe again, to avenge the deaths of those who lost their lives on September 11, 2001, and send a message to the Muslim world. But we believed it was really just a war to make war, and for others, to make money.

If winning meant destroying the government of Saddam Hussein, the war in Iraq was a success. But in all other ways, it was much more than just a failure. It was the beginning of the end of "peace in our time." The war in Iraq tarnished America's image abroad, destabilized the Middle East, and incited anti-American sentiment in the Muslim world. One company, Kellogg Brown and Root, a subsidiary of Halliburton, once run by Dick Cheney prior to his becoming vice president, was awarded $39.5 billion in government contracts during the Iraq War.

There were times when the only passion I could muster toward the war was anger. A kind of anger that if it isn't checked becomes rage. I had argued with Leigh about his decision to join the military in the first place and played every mother card in the deck. I shed tears on the "What about us left here to do nothing but worry" theme. All to no avail. I ran hot and cold, seeking whatever it was going to take to dissuade Leigh, until he finally said, "You and Dad always talk about the importance of public service. My grandparents were both governors. Dad was a supreme court justice. So now it's my turn." Checkmate. There really was nothing more I could say.

Friends and acquaintances offered bland reassurances: "No need to worry. He'll be fine." Most of the people I knew had never sent a child to war. Their children were bound for lives in banking, law, medicine, or perhaps best of all, taking over the businesses that their great-grandfathers had started.

"With all your connections, why in the world would Leigh join the army? Somebody would have hired him right here at home," one acquaintance said. Most days I was just too tired to argue.

"BUSY HANDS MAKE for happy hands," Mama used to say. "Keep you out of mischief." Perhaps busy hands will take my mind off the war, I thought. I pulled out some cardboard boxes from the back of my closet I hadn't seen in years. One of them was sealed. A stick-on tag on top said there were photos inside.

"I found this today." I showed Mark a photo when he came home. "It was like Mama was sending me a message. I couldn't believe what I saw. All I could do was cry."

Mama was standing on a military parade ground flanked by a uniformed officer of the Alabama National Guard. She was reviewing her troops. She was their governor and commander in chief. As I held the photo in my hands, I began to think of the pride Mama would have had in her grandson's call to serve.

"Mama, I wish you had lived long enough to see Leigh in his uniform," I said to myself.

I became determined to spend my time honoring our soldiers, praying for their safe return, engaging friends and family to send parcels and letters to Leigh and the members of his platoon and reading his letters from Baghdad. I wanted others like me, who never thought about war, to read letters from someone they knew, a childhood playmate, the boy that sat next to their daughter in school, a kid that waved when they drove by.

> We had the first casualty in our battalion. He had a wife and four children. Mom, he was killed on your birthday.

> ———

> A lot of our soldiers are teenagers. You have to be at least nineteen to operate a .50 caliber machine gun. I had to leave my operator behind. He is eighteen.

> ———

> A friend of mine was killed today. He was in 2nd platoon. We secured the area so the medevac could land. He had

been shot in the head. He died before they landed. He had an eleven-year-old son.

———

I was on patrol in Sadr City. I had my interpreter with me. We stopped a man who was walking toward us. It looked like he wanted to talk, but he wouldn't say anything. He whispered to my interpreter to follow him to his house. When we got inside, the man broke down and started crying. He told me his two sons had been beheaded two weeks ago. He was afraid that if anyone saw him talking to us, he would be next.

———

We were setting up a perimeter for a medical unit in Sadr City. There were tons of children that flocked to the trucks once they saw us there. They know that Americans are known for passing out toys and candy. The bigger kids will use the younger kids as a fortification to get close to our trucks to lob a grenade inside the turret. So, we are constantly telling them to get back. At one point I got out of my truck. I noticed this one little girl. She kept wanting to play guess which hand with a marble she had. We would play; then she would get knocked out of the way by the larger kids. After being outside for a while, I got back in the truck. I lost sight of her. Then I saw her coming outside a house with a tray of water in her hands. I got back out of my truck and she gave me some water to drink. I reluctantly drank it knowing the water probably was not purified. Then she made sure she went to the other trucks and gave them a glass, as well. I was amazed at the kindness of this little girl.

———

I had a big bag of candy under the seat. I knew I would be playing with fire if I got out of the vehicle with candy in my hand but I wanted to give it to the little girl. She was scared when I motioned her to come to my truck. There was an Iraqi man standing not far from me. I managed to explain to him that I wanted to give her the bag of candy. We got the candy to her and watched until she got to her house. That man and I were enemies in the midst of a war, but for that moment we were on the same team.

———

One hundred fourteen soldiers were killed this month. Forty of them were between the ages of 18 and 21.

———

There were two suicide bombings in a market in Sadr City today. They strapped bombs on two mentally challenged women and told them to walk around. When they got in the middle of a lot of people, the bombs were remotely detonated.

Twenty thousand soldiers were deployed to Iraq in what was referred to as the Surge, in January and February of 2007. Leigh was one of them. During the fifteen months he was there, 7,085 soldiers were wounded and 867 soldiers were killed. There were no ticker-tape parades for those who returned. It was over and forgotten.

I used to wonder how can there be dignity in the death of an American soldier who dies in the midst of an unjust war. But for those mothers who lay flowers on the graves of their sons and daughters who died in Iraq, perhaps dignity is all that is left. And who are we to think less of their grief than the grief of those who lay flowers on the tombs of heroes who died to protect American liberty and justice for all?

28

Back to the Bridge

Alone we can do so little; together we can do so much.

—*Helen Keller*

On August 28, 1963, Dr. Martin Luther King Jr. stood on the steps of the Lincoln Memorial and spoke to the heart of America. It was one of his finest moments. He told America, "I have a dream that my four little children will one day live in a nation where they will not be judged by the color of their skin but by the content of their character. I have a dream. I have a dream that one day in Alabama, with its vicious racists, with its governor having his lips dripping with the words of interposition and nullification, one day right there in Alabama little black boys and black girls will be able to join hands with little white boys and white girls as sisters and brothers."

It was March 2015. I thought of King's speech as thousands of people marched up Dexter Avenue to the Alabama state capitol

Me and Donzaleigh Abernathy at the Faith and Politics Civil Rights Pilgrimage, March 2017.

for the fiftieth anniversary of the Selma to Montgomery march. Dr. King's daughter Bernice and I held hands as we stood on the steps of the Alabama capitol as the marchers approached.

I could not help but wonder how the course of history might have been changed if Martin Luther King and Daddy had known that one day, right down here in Alabama, that little black girl and that little white girl holding hands would be their own daughters.

ON MARCH 8, members of a congressional delegation took their seats beneath a tent in front of the Alabama capitol. John Lewis and I sat together on the street-level plaza of the capitol grounds.

We were gathered there to celebrate and honor the memory of the Selma to Montgomery march.

The ground under my feet was where my past resided, reminding me of the life I had lived: floats and waving beauty queens, bands and majorettes, adoring crowds at five Wallace inaugurations. I thought of Daddy's words: "Segregation now, segregation tomorrow, and segregation forever" and the malevolent roars that followed. And I also remembered the mourning crowds of whites and blacks, twice gathered and inching along for hours, some beneath the stars, to pay their respects to the memory of my mother and father whose bodies lay in state in the capitol rotunda. I remembered taking Mark to meet Daddy beneath a Confederate flag waving high atop the capitol dome.

John and I sat together on what was hallowed and embattled American ground. It was a place of opportunity for me to do for John what he did for me on the day we crossed the Edmund Pettus Bridge.

John smiled and nodded at me as he adjusted the lectern microphone.

"On March the 25 of 1965, as Ralph Abernathy, Juanita Abernathy, Martin Luther King, John Lewis, and thousands more gathered in the shadow of this capitol, there was never an opportunity to address their concerns or state their grievances to the one person who could have changed the course of American history then and there," I began.

> For Governor Wallace watched through a window in the privacy of his office, while others persevered and changed the history of America without him.

Today, we must not allow others to make the right choices for us. We must have courage each day to stand up for equality and the rights of all Americans. We must lead by example and live our lives with inspiration, always aspiring to make the choices that lead us to higher ground, that guide us to understanding and purpose of not just who we are but who we can become.

An opportunity for each of you, an obligation for all of us, to see others, feel others, and celebrate others, respecting their humanity for who they are. Working each day to inspire the nobility that lies in the heart of each of us. How can Americans reach for higher ground if we do not inspire others with what we do? We must promise that when we say all men are created equal, it means something. Tolerance must be more than what we believe, it must be what we live, and leading by example is what we must do. Tolerance does not always mean agreement, but tolerance always requires understanding and compassion for others.

I am most thankful for the life and inspiration of Congressman John Lewis. And standing here by his side, there now comes an opportunity for me, in some small measure, to return to you what you gave to me as we stood together on the Edmund Pettus Bridge.

Fifty years ago, you stood here in front of your state capitol and sought an opportunity as a citizen of Alabama to be recognized and heard by your governor and he refused. But today as his daughter and as a person of my own, I want to do for you what my father should have done and recognize you for your humanity and for your dignity as a child of God, as a person of goodwill and character, and as a fellow Alabamian, and say, welcome home.

JOHN AND I held hands as we walked to the Civil Rights Memorial several blocks away. In the midst of a stark and solemn plaza stands a black granite wall engraved with Martin Luther King's paraphrase of Amos 5:24: We will not be satisfied "until justice rolls down like waters and righteousness like a mighty stream." In front of it, an inverted black granite cone rises from the ground. On its flat top, names of the martyrs of the civil rights

Congressman John Lewis, me, and Mark on the
Edmund Pettus Bridge in Selma, Alabama, 2018.

movement are etched like the hands of a clock, marking moments we should never forget.

John and I put our hands on the tabletop. The water that flows across the memorial rippled over our hands. Our fingers touched. The water flowed over the names of those who died, then into the ground to find its way to the Alabama River. It would flow beneath the Edmund Pettus Bridge where we had found each another. It would flow south to the Delta into Mobile Bay and out into the Gulf.

ON MARCH 8, 2017, following a dinner at the Alabama State Archives in Montgomery, I spoke to a congressional delegation, including Congressman Lewis.

> While there is never a bad time to honor the struggle for civil rights in American history, there is no better time than now to heed the call for freedom and justice for all that was the hallmark of the civil rights movement . . .
>
> When we say all men are created equal, it means something, protects something and encourages us to embrace the belief that the diversity among us has nothing to do with equality but has everything to do with strength.
>
> There are lessons to be learned along the roadways that others have traveled in pursuit of their dreams of enjoying the full measure of equality. There are great moments in history when men, women, and children stood their ground to demand the rights that were

guaranteed to them. And now is the time to fulfill the promise we pledge each time the American flag goes by.

There is never a bad time for us to engage in acts of public service that create opportunities for enlightenment and change. For we cannot expect the next generation of Americans to do something to change the world if we do nothing to recognize our individual obligations to service.

Following my speech, I took a seat on the front row of the auditorium as John and a moderator came to the stage and sat down side by side. After several general comments, the moderator turned to John and asked him to reflect on Daddy's life, what legacies he left behind.

John paused, as if he were gathering his thoughts, before speaking. He turned in his chair and pointed a finger directly at me. For a moment, it was as if all of the oxygen had been sucked from the room.

"How could I say anything bad about George Wallace, when this is his daughter?" he said.

With those words, John Lewis, who grew up in Troy, who had lived just thirty-eight miles from me when we were young, allowed me to realize that I was perhaps Daddy's most important legacy of all.

AFTERWORD

We are born in moments that turn to days then months and years of dawns of hope and sunsets of despair. But the moments we should remember first are those of conquering our fears, standing our ground, sacrificing for someone we love, and standing up for the rights of a perfect stranger because it is the right and righteous thing to do.

I discovered my true self while traveling along the broken road. I learned that breaking away from a painful past is not always easy, but it is always right. And I found my voice for the benefit of history, for myself, my husband Mark, and our two sons, Leigh and Burns.

When I was a young girl, I rode on the wings of the politics of hate and fear as it carried me away from my childhood and conquered my dream of a simple life. But through it all, I refused to lose faith in my hope that one day my life would count for something. And I wanted to be remembered for who I was rather than who I belonged to.

The broken road set me free. It helped me to better understand the past, what made us, and who we are. And it taught me that my life could be measured not from where I came from but where I was going, and to believe that each of us has the power to change first our own lives and then the lives of others.

Several years ago, my son Burns came rushing through our back door. He was returning from a large business conference in Gulf Shores, Alabama. "Mom," he said, "I was standing in the middle of a reception when a man walked up to me. He looked at the name badge on my coat, *Morgan Burns Kennedy.* 'I know who you are,' he said. 'You are Peggy Wallace Kennedy's son, aren't you? Not Dad, not Paw Paw or Mawmaw Lurleen, just you!'"

Burns wrapped his arms around me for a lingering hug. "You made it, Mom, you made it," he said.

The inscription on the Statue of Liberty reads: "Give me your tired, your poor, / Your huddled masses yearning to breathe free, / The wretched refuse of your teeming shore. / Send these the homeless, tempest-tost to me, / I lift up my lamp beside the golden door!"

That is the American promise that men and women long for, that our sons and daughters fight for, and what our sense of morality should stand for. It is an American dream that gives rise to heartfelt moments that encourage us to believe that each of us has a personal obligation to live in the present and work each day for the promise of a more just America where life, liberty, and the pursuit of happiness remains.

The mothers, fathers, daughters, and sons of the civil rights movement of the 1950s and beyond never wavered in their belief that justice would come. And they prayed for the day when the fair winds of freedom and following seas would carry them to the shores of a life without fear and a heart of purpose.

There is power in confidence, in feeling loved and respected for who you are and what you believe; it is the reaching out and touching a soul that brings out the humanity of others. And there are moments in all of our lives when the future can become more important than the past, where "I shall overcome" becomes "I have overcome."

Now is the time for Americans to hold hands with one another rather than holding down the inherent rights of the common man. For no one can ever measure the true worth of a mended heart that beats because someone cared. How can our sons and daughters stand on mountaintops if we do not teach them how to climb? If we live a life of purpose and hope, our voices will be heard and we will never have to think about the cost of a lost chance to say the right thing or stand up and be counted.

It's like what Mamaw said to me after Mama died: "Peggy Sue, nobody is given the same opportunities in life but if we work hard and do right, we can make opportunities of our own. Your mama showed me that." She said, "Now go out back and tell Mr. Henry to stop what he's doing so he can ride us up by the broken road."

My family. Back row, left to right: Morgan Burns Kennedy and Leigh Chancellor Kennedy. Front row, left to right: Hannah Torbert Kennedy (wife of Burns Kennedy), Justice H. Mark Kennedy, Peggy Wallace Kennedy, Maggie Rose Kennedy (granddaughter), and Stephanie Rion Kennedy (wife of Leigh Kennedy).

ACKNOWLEDGMENTS

My journey along the the broken road began when I was young. It just took me a lifetime to reunite with it, understand it, and recognize those who joined me on my journey.

With love:
To my husband of forty-six years, Mark, I could not have taken this journey without you. Your love, your patience, and your talent of envisioning scenes with words helped bring the story to life. Such as what Mamaw says to Daddy after Mother's inauguration: "Well, George, this is for sure one time you can thank Lurleen for keeping a roof over your head and food on the table. Can't be any arguing about that anymore, now can there?"

To recognize:
My parents, George and Lurleen Burns Wallace; my maternal grandparents, Estelle Burns and Henry Morgan Burns; my son Army Major Leigh Chancellor Kennedy and his wife, Stephanie; my son Morgan Burns Kennedy and his wife, Hannah; our

incredible granddaughter, Maggie Rose; and Mark's parents, Douglas and Marjorie Kennedy.

Memories:

"I told you, you should write a book one day," Mark's mother once said.

My uncle Gerald, who meant so much to me and to Mark, is with me in spirit, still calling me "Peggy Sue" with a larger-than-life smile. His daughters, Debbie and Sherry, who love to tell stories about their dad.

My fond memories of the bigger-than-life stories of Cornelia Wallace and her mother, "Big Ruby," always make me smile.

Daddy and Mama's security details and their wives, who protected us, loved us, and were part of our family.

My constant light at the end of life's tunnels, my dearest friend, Marianne Fulford.

My friends of many years, my Bellingrath Junior High School girls, the "BG's," who make me feel young again, and remind me of the better part of my past, including my precious friend, Janie.

I learned what love through forgiveness meant when Congressman John Lewis held my hand, called me "sister," and walked with me across the Edmund Pettus Bridge in Selma, Alabama.

The daughters of the civil rights movement: Kerry Kennedy, Donzaleigh Abernathy, Reverend Bernice King, Lynda Johnson Robb, and Luci Baines Johnson, who recognized me as one of their own.

My friend, Mary Luizzo Lilleboe, who is very special to me.

To all our friends, coworkers, supporters, law clerks, court reporters, judicial assistants, judges and justices, best friends and casual friends, and all of my fellow Alabamians who still walk up to me to share stories about Mama and Daddy, we thank you.

To so many others who befriended me, came to know me, and loved and encouraged me along the way, you will always inspire me to keep seeking higher ground.

To my literary agent, Gail Ross, and all her work to find *The Broken Road* a home, we are most grateful.

To my editor, Kenny Wapner, for all your advice, your insightful suggestions, and your support throughout. You made the book better.

To the author of the foreword, Dr. Wayne Flynt, thank you for your friendship and your contribution to the truth of *The Broken Road*.

Most importantly, my heartfelt thanks to my publisher, Bloomsbury USA, and especially to Nancy Miller, who believed in me and in my journey along the broken road. I am forever grateful. To all of you, my Bloomsbury family, your compassion, wisdom, and your talent make this story more than I could ever have dreamed it would be.

INDEX

Note: page numbers in italics refer to figures.

A NOTE ON THE AUTHORS

Peggy Wallace Kennedy is a nationally recognized speaker, lecturer, and writer. Her father and mother, George and Lurleen Wallace, were both governors of Alabama. She has been honored by, among other groups, the Southern Christian Leadership Conference, the Martin Luther King Commission, and the Emmett Till Legacy Foundation, and has received the Woman of Courage, Human Rights, and Rosa Parks Legacy Awards. Her dedication to racial reconciliation offers hope for change in a divided America. She lives in Montgomery, Alabama.

Justice H. Mark Kennedy, Peggy's husband of forty-five years, has served as a judge for more than two decades, including two terms as a justice of the Supreme Court of Alabama. Together they have two sons.